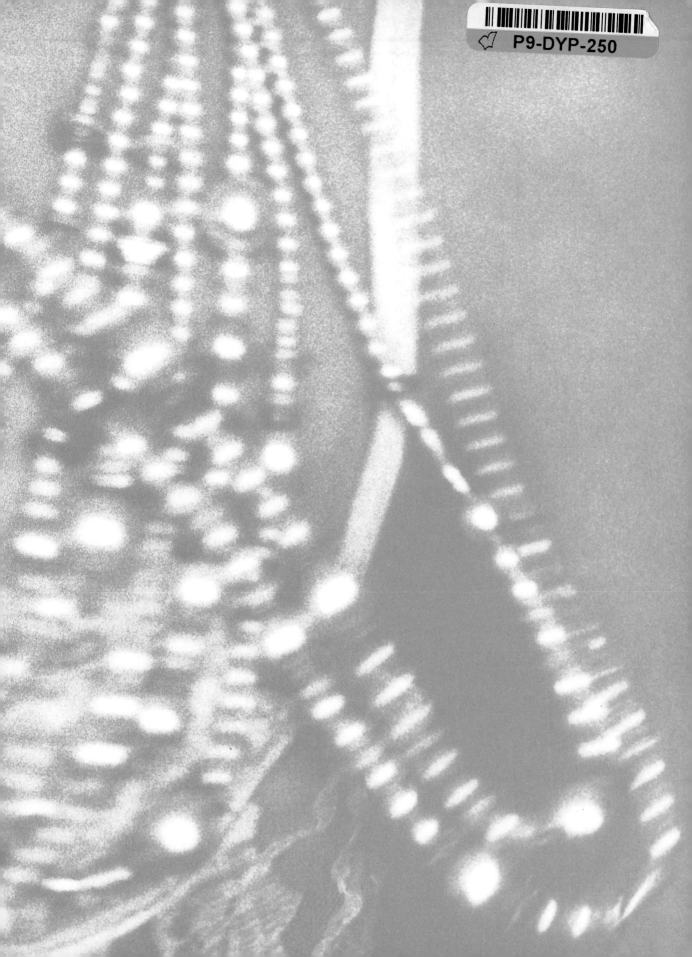

PEOPLE & PEARLS

The Magic Endures

PEOPLE
&PEARLS

The Magic Endures

KI HACKNEY AND DIANA EDKINS

HarperCollinsPublishers

EDITOR: JOSEPH MONTEBELLO

DESIGNER: JOEL AVIROM

DESIGN ASSISTANTS: MEGHAN DAY HEALEY AND JASON SNYDER

PAGE i: This Man Ray photograph of his mistress Kiki de Montparnasse, a celebrated Parisian dancer and artist's model in the 1920s, is from his surrealistic film called *L'Étoile de Mer* (1928). The voluptuous, oversized "pearls" highlighting Kiki's neck are, in reality, painted beads of glass.

PAGES ii—iii: Karl Lagerfeld captures the sensuality of a surplus of pearls in his photograph of model Brandy luxuriating in pearls from his spring-summer 1995 ready-to-wear collection for Chanel.

PAGE vi: Uma Thurman, resplendent in an 8.5 mm—8 mm necklace and stud earrings from Mikimoto, recalled the halcyon days of Hollywood in this January 1996 cover shot for *Vanity Fair* magazine. A 16-inch strand—the shortest Mikimoto offers—was customized to create the choker effect.

HarperCollins books may be purchased for educational, business, or sales promotional use. For information please write: Special Markets Department, HarperCollins Publishers Inc., 10 East 53rd Street, New York, NY 10022.

FIRST EDITION 2000

Printed on acid-free paper

Library of Congress Cataloging-in-Publication Data

Hackney, Ki.
    People and pearls ; the magic endures / Ki Hackney and Diana Edkins,—1st ed.
      p. cm.
    Includes bibliographical references.
    ISBN 0-06-019331-X
     1. Pearls. 2. Fashion—History.   I. Edkins, Diana. II. Title.

GT2255 .H33 2000
391.7—dc21

                         00-038433

00 01 02 03 04 10 9 8 7 6 5 4 3 2 1

This book is dedicated to our daughters,
Caroline, Christina, and Joanna,
and to our husbands, Carl and Philip,
for their unwavering support and their
absolute belief in the power of pearls.

ONTENTS

$\mathcal{A}$CKNOWLEDGMENTS

Without the vision and commitment of Joseph Montebello, Joel Avirom, Janis A. Donnaud, and Helen F. Pratt this book would not exist. We offer our thanks to John Haffner-Layden for his guidance, our gratitude to all the photographers for their cooperation, and our appreciation to the following:

Bob Adelman, Ray Aghayan, Pierre Appraxime, Salvador Assael, Mouna Al-Ayoub, Letitia Baldrige, Ivan Bart, Timothy Baum, Dierdre Baxter, Gigi Benson, Lenore Benson, Viren Bhagat, Catherine Bigwood, Kevin Bisch, Jim Black, Alison Bond, Janet Borden, Amanda Bowman, Barbara Taylor Bradford, Ron Brenne, Chris Brenner, Jeryl Brenner, Jennifer Bressler, Tom Britt, Nan Bush, Meredith Cabe, John Cantrell, Paul Cavaco, Carrie Chalmers, Sheila Chefetz, Bob Cosenza, David Patrick Columbia, Norman Currie, Sal Daselva, Bart Delia, Virginia Dodier, Carrie Donovan, Valerie Duport, Isabelle Eaton, Joe Enos, Ralph Esmerian, Joe Eula, David Fahey, Pamela Fiori, Nian Fish, Marilise Flusser, Carolee Friedlander, Etta Froio, Philippe Garner, Marika Genty, John Gibbons, Cécile Goddet, Andrea Goldfein, Heinrich Graf von Spreti, Carol Taylor Gray, Lee Gruzen, C.Z. Guest, Pia Halloran, G. Ray Hawkins, Meghan Day Healey, Chris Hewitt, Jenni Holder, Margaret Hoisik, Christopher Holm, Edwynn Houk, Aude Bronson-Howard, Ed Johnson, Jim Johnson, Joyce Jonas, Lydia Cresswell-Jones, Anne Jouvenal, Clive Kandel, Goro Kamata, Sudhir Kasliwal, Nan Kempner, Elizabeth Kerr, James Kilvington, William Sanford King, Stephen Kiviat, Christina Krupka, Carol Lalli, Eleanor Lambert, Ward Landrigan, Kenneth Jay Lane, Janet Lehr, Fred Leighton, Trisha and David Lown, Nicholas Luchsinger, Bob Mackie, Devin Macnow, Barbara Mancuso, Ron Mandelbaum, Lys Marigold, Christophe Mauberret, Steven Mazzara, Everett McCarver, Robert McElroy, Bill McTighe, Sylvia Meixner, John Melick, L. Scott Miller, Andrea Modica, Seamus Mullarkey, Jessica Murray, Herbert Nass, Mimi di Nescemi, Ryl Norquist, Frank Newbold, Gillian and Uwe Siemon-Netto, Bob Newey, Mitchell Owens, Jim Oxnam, Terence Pepper, Neal Peters, Bill Powers, Timothy Priano, Amelia Prounis, Yves Rambaud, Richard Raziniski, Allen Reuben, Anise Richey, Linda Ritter, Julie Saul, Michael Senft, Mary Beth Shea, Eveline Sievi, Caroline Simonelli, Jeffrey Smith, Carlota Woolworth Stahl, Sandy Starkman, Michael Stier, Michael Ward Stout, William H. Summers, André Leon Talley, Simon Teakle, Arlette Thebault, Susan Train, Hugo Vickers, Tammy Walker, Jo Wallace, Christopher Walling, June Weir, Kathryn Wilson, Virginia Witbeck, Mitchell Wolfson, Jr., Colin Woodhead, and Eric Young.

INTRODUCTION

HAVE YOU EVER FOUND YOURSELF drawn to someone who was wearing pearls? You might be captivated by someone else wearing diamonds, but it's the diamonds that sparkle. When a woman wears pearls, it is she who shines. Pearls complement a woman in whatever she is doing. They become part of her, not something worn by her. With quiet grace and seductive allure, pearls help a woman convey who she is, or who she wants to be.

The pearls people select and the ways they dress with them reveal a good bit about their wearers, including the times in which they live, and a lot about style. For example, some women, such as Brooke Astor, C.Z. Guest, and England's Queen Mother, have grown up in the tradition of pearls, and their trademark pearls have long been emblematic of their personal loyalties to traditional society. In contrast, Josephine Baker's costumes in the 1920s made pearls part of her public persona, but to very different effect. The dramatic cascades of the sensuous gems that Baker wore symbolized a heady world of change that was Paris after the turn of the century. More familiar today, though, are those who wear pearls on certain occasions, for particular effects. New York fashion consultant Marilise Flusser affirms the practice of wearing pearls for psychological support and image: "Pearls are the ultimate power accessory. There is nothing more hip than wearing a beautiful pearl necklace with a clean white T-shirt. And when you put on a Chanel suit and pearls, no one can criticize you. You become unassailable."

People & Pearls: The Magic Endures is an exploration of the intimate connection between people and pearls. It is not a definitive treatise on this oldest of gems. Nor is it a biographical anthology of pearl wearers throughout time. While we have attempted to reveal the pertinent facts about pearls, illustrate different types of pearls, highlight a few of the important

One hundred and fifty strings of 100 egg-shaped pearls (3x2mm) each can be threaded through the 15k gold disk clasp and adjusted "to balance the necklace between the front and the back of the body," says jeweler and sculptor Ibu Poilane. Her inspiration for the necklace: the sensuality of 150,000 pearls undulating against the skin. Karl Lagerfeld broke with tradition and accessorized some of the models for his fall-winter 1998–1999 couture collection for Chanel with Ibu's modern take on a luxurious pearl rope.

historic pearls and pearl wearers, our vision is a bit more elusive, more ethereal, and definitely more quirky.

Pearls have power. We wanted to create a visual and personal book that captures this power and probes the elusive relationship between people and pearls. Our hope is that you will come to learn that the pearl is more than a mere adornment and that the history of pearls is not simply a chronicle of fashion or jewelry, but the story of a gem whose place in time is the result of its myriad, and often mythical, qualities. In the process, you will become acquainted with some of the most picturesque characters throughout civilization, whose extraordinary lives have lent an inimitable texture to our everlasting passion for pearls.

The book is a union of significant portraits—some never before published—and the history of the world's oldest gem as told through the lives of some of the world's most powerful, beguiling, and creative men and women who have pursued pearls. Each chapter introduces readers to a different group of pearl wearers and explores the varied roles that the pearl has played over time for that group. We begin with "Innocents"—an exploration of pearls as a traditional offering in honor of the physical and spiritual celebrations of youth and innocence (a stretch that we consider starts at birth and ends at marriage). Next, in "Lords and Lovers," we pay tribute to the royal heritage of pearls. This chapter conveniently highlights the periods of rich pearl trade and usage and some of their more absorbing characters. We look at the Renaissance, czarist Russia, prerevolutionary France, Mughal India, the Middle Eastern foundation of pearls, and the legacy of pearls within and surrounding the British Empire. The traditional ruling-class command of pearls established a desirability and social code for pearls that continues to this day. Rich or poor, all good "Traditionalists" wear pearls as a badge of their belief in solid values, and anyone wearing pearls projects an aura of elegance and self-possession, as well as a sensuousness that is unknown in other gemstones. In *People & Pearls: The Magic Endures* we wanted to explore this well-known, yet intangible force that continues to drive the desire for pearls. Quite the opposite of the traditionalist approach is that of the "Dream Makers"—those who use pearls to communicate the wildly artistic side of their personalities. Their tool kit for self-expression is the rich world of jewelry and fantasy, and as the subjects step out of tradition and into their highly individual, idiosyncratic visions, they make use of every sort of pearl item, from a single-strand choker or cascade of ropes to a pearl-embroidered chemise or headdress. Adding to the mysterious draw of pearls is the abandon with which they can be used—the wildly artistic tool kit from the most imaginative headpiece or other decorative apparel to the boldest bracelet. Front and center in this chapter, and setting the stage for the pearl icons and the "Eternal Lights" of pearls, are Coco Chanel and Diana Vreeland. Coco Chanel was herself a dramatic package with hats, glasses, matched cuff bracelets, and ropes and ropes of pearls with her comfortable suits and trousers by day and pearls draped over her shoulders and down her back in the evening. While she might have overstated the look for effect, she made her point, and women all over the world have adopted and adapted the Chanel look. In addition to her stream-lined couture, Mademoiselle Chanel's populist appeal also stemmed from her delight in mixing fake jewelry with the finest bijoux. In doing so, she raised the status of imitation pearls and the new cultured varieties, and legitimized their day-to-day use. Thanks to Coco Chanel, real or fake, pearls are a safe bet.

Mademoiselle Chanel ushered in a fashion aesthetic that, in its simplicity, resonates with women today. Diana Vreeland, who inherited Coco Chanel's everyday pearl earrings, also used hyperbole to distill her unique vision of couture both in her striking editorials and by personal example. Mrs. Vreeland and Mademoiselle Chanel are also guiding lights for the final chapters which address the icons of pearls—the women and their pearls who have provided everlasting images of pearls for modern times. "The Untouchables" are the icons with incomparable flair, charisma, and the power of the media behind them. Grace Kelly, Jackie Onassis, and Princess Diana

At a 1996 White House power lunch, this trio of high-profile women had at least one thing in common: creamy white pearls. Each woman had opted for the safety of pearls that managed to transmit her individual sense of style. *Vogue* editor in chief Anna Wintour explained the coincidence to reporter Anna Stewart: "You can't really think of three more different women, but we all reached for our pearls this morning," she said, pointing out that with pearls, "you just can't go wrong. I'd love to have what Diana's wearing. Those are very real and expensive. Hillary's are very classic. Mine are baroque and lighter." The fashion style broker's comment underscored a truth about pearls: they are an all-purpose accessory possessing enigmatic power.

used pearls in a vocabulary that remains understandable and useful to people everywhere, no matter how creative or elite the original wrapping. And adding closure to the principal theme of this book—the relationship between people and pearls—are the "Eternal Lights." The images on these pages are meant to salute not only the depth of character that develops over time and the wisdom of age, but the timeless richness of the pearl.

By seeing how each group wears pearls, readers will come to understand the rich and complex appeal of these natural gems and be inspired by the ways history's luminaries have used pearls to adorn themselves. Put simply, we hope that this book does two things: delve through time to reveal the many symbolic, decorative, and even economic functions that the pearl has played in the drama of history, and encourage readers to expand their personal styles as they page through the work of some of the world's most celebrated photographers and painters. With this latter goal in mind, we have concluded *People & Pearls: The Magic Endures* with a consumer guide of practical information about pearls, including a glossary of pearl-related terms, and how and where to buy them—whether they be the most luxurious, sought-after natural and cultured varieties or outrageous fakes. While utilitarian in nature, it is the touchdown for our exploration of the somewhat fantasmagoric relationship between people and pearls. On a pragmatic level, this very businesslike information is a counterpoint to the elusive connection between people and their pearls and helps explain why someone like astroanalyst and author Albert Clayton Gaulden, at a turning point in his life in 1980, spent his last five hundred dollars on a pearl necklace for Mary, one of his sisters. "She is overweight and, like me, she was not one of the beauties of the family. I wanted her to feel luxurious and elegant and touched by me in a way she never had been. She wears them to church as if she were the queen of the neighboring farmers' wives in Alabama, and she still wears those pearls to bed, because she feels special enough to have them." Also, it explains why serious jewelry collector Marcia Rubin, the widow of a successful New York real estate investor , used to sleep in her favorite pair of pearl-and-diamond bracelets—the sale of which she originally usurped, at eighty-six thousand dollars each, during a trunk showing of designer Henry Dunay's jewelry at McCarver and Moser in Sarasota, so that no other woman could have even one of them. People and their pearls certainly constitute a union that fascinates and endures.

— *Ki Hackney and Diana Edkins*

PEOPLE & PEARLS

The Magic Endures

A QUIRK

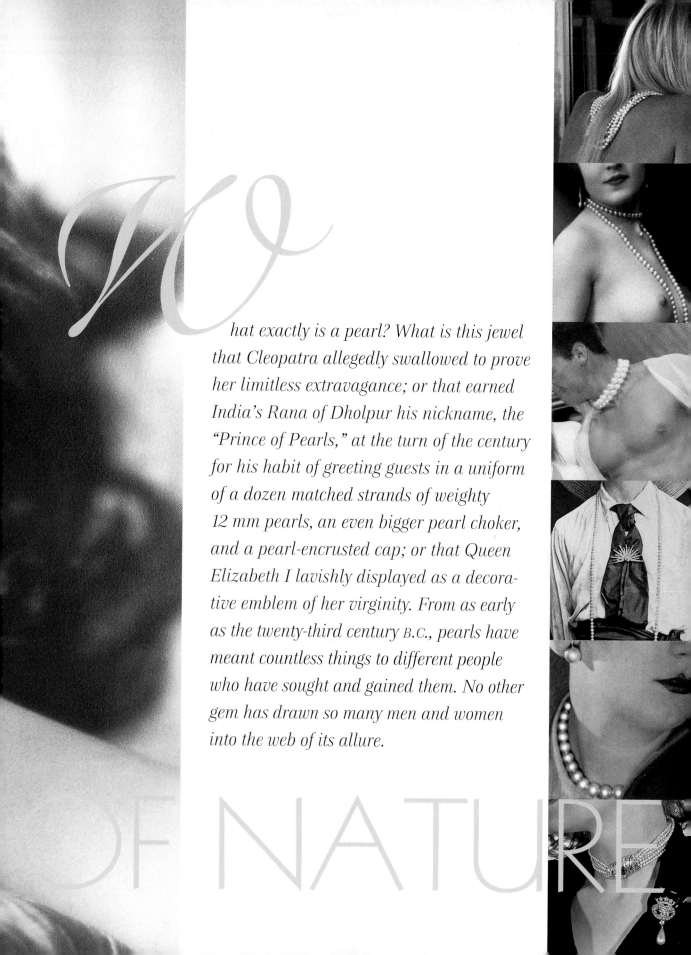

*W*hat exactly is a pearl? What is this jewel that Cleopatra allegedly swallowed to prove her limitless extravagance; or that earned India's Rana of Dholpur his nickname, the "Prince of Pearls," at the turn of the century for his habit of greeting guests in a uniform of a dozen matched strands of weighty 12 mm pearls, an even bigger pearl choker, and a pearl-encrusted cap; or that Queen Elizabeth I lavishly displayed as a decorative emblem of her virginity. From as early as the twenty-third century B.C., pearls have meant countless things to different people who have sought and gained them. No other gem has drawn so many men and women into the web of its allure.

OF NATURE

The ancient origins of the word itself lend a clue to the pearl's enduring appeal. In classic Sanskrit literature of the first century of the Christian Era, pearls were referred to as *mukta,* or "the pure." In fact, the pearl's very creation and appearance suggest the purity that has been so highly prized over time and across cultures.

Its soft contour, luminescence, and dewy white coloration, even its watery home, establish the pearl as a natural metaphor for purity. And unlike other gemstones, pearls need no cutting, faceting, or polishing to bring out their splendor. Iridescence is this gem's birthright.

Despite their association with purity and natural perfection, pearls are actually a quirk of nature—a fortuitous by-product of the defense systems of both saltwater and freshwater mollusks in action. Although there are thousands of different species of mollusks, only a few—mostly saltwater oysters and freshwater mussels—produce pearls that find their way into some of the world's most coveted jewelry.

As a humble mollusk feeds, it draws through its shell a constant flow of water, along with sand, parasites, and other particles that are caught in the wake. Although the shell of a mollusk provides a sturdy housing and the mother-of-pearl lining a clean environment, the animal's soft tissue is vulnerable to harmful invaders that enter the shell during the circulation of water. When a foreign object, such as a piece of shell or a parasite, enters and cannot be expelled, the mollusk protects itself from injury by sealing the intruder in a cocoon of conchiolin, a substance that neutralizes the irritant and triggers the production of nacre. Nacre, a pale substance composed of microscopic calcium carbonate crystals, is the same lustrous coating known as mother-of-pearl when it sheaths the inside of these pearl-producing mollusk shells. The aggrieved mollusk continues to cover the irritant with layer upon layer of nacre for a period that can extend to many years. These layers harden to form a pearl. Light traveling through the overlapping layers of nacre is refracted and creates the prismatic rainbow effect that uniquely characterizes a pearl's outer appearance.

When a pearl is born in this spontaneous fashion, it is known as a natural pearl, and natural pearls are extremely rare. The demand for pearls has long since exceeded the supply from natural sources. Overfishing, industrialization, and pollution have destroyed most of the natural pearl beds that were once so plentiful.

The sources for splendid pearls have shifted over time, depending on the tides of nature and more so on the industry of man. The Per-

PAGE 2: Claudette Colbert, as Cleopatra, in Cecil B. DeMille's 1934 classic film about the ruler who drank her pearl earring, dissolved in a glass of wine, to provide her lover, Mark Antony, with a more extravagant meal than he could reciprocate. The film star's dramatic rings and bracelets not only echo the legendary Cleopatra's passion for pearls, they are lustrous examples of the Hollywood brand of bold jewelry that helped launch America as a rich source of style and chic.

sian Gulf, particularly the Bay of Bahrain, supplied most of the natural pearls in antiquity. The other important sources are in that part of the world—the Gulf of Mannar waters off the coast of Ceylon (Sri Lanka) and the Arab countries bordering the Red Sea. Many of the rivers and streams of Europe were abundant with pearl-bearing mussels. Legend contends that Julius Caesar invaded Scotland in order to obtain the acclaimed pink pearls.

Even the United States had its share of pearl treasures. A freshwater pearl necklace, dating back almost 3,000 years, was unearthed at the Hopewell Indian burial ground in Ohio. Two of the most important American pearls were plucked from the streams near Paterson, New Jersey, in early 1897. The first, weighing nearly 400 grains (100 carats), was spoiled by a shoemaker who found it in the stream near his home. Unaware that a gem was nestled in the mussels that he was preparing for his meal, he fried the pearl. The second, a lustrous 13-carat pink pearl weighing 93 grains was discovered a few days later in the same area by a local carpenter. Charles Tiffany bought the pearl for $1,500. Unable to sell it in New York, Tiffany & Co. sold the American pearl to a gem dealer in Paris for 12,500 francs, and the dealer found a buyer in the wife of Napoléon III. In honor of the great beauty of both the pearl and Empress Eugénie, this historic pearl, valued at about $10,000 at the turn of the century, is formally known as the "Queen Pearl."

While pearls were found throughout the United States, from Maine to Ohio, Colorado, and California, they were particularly plentiful in the Mississippi Valley, extending north into Minnesota and Wisconsin, and south to Tennessee. The Baja peninsula in Mexico was known for radiant black pearls, and Venezuela and Panama were rich sources for dazzling white pearls comparable to those found in ancient Ceylon and Persia. In China pearls were fished from the freshwater rivers and streams, while coastal seawater provided Japan with its resource for pearl-bearing mollusks. Finally, Australia, home of the largest pearl-bearing oyster, has also played a critical role in the story of pearls.

Since the turn of the twentieth century human intervention has helped to create a new supply of mollusk-born gems, called cultured pearls. Pearl culturing centers on the process of artificially implanting an irritant to provoke the mollusk into releasing the nacreous coating that produces a pearl. The Chinese understood the principle as early as the eighth century A.D. Knowing that a mollusk would coat anything in its shell with nacre, they placed small lead Buddhas inside the shells to trigger the flow of nacre, which produced pearl-covered figures.

While their female companion prefers the flash of diamonds, these men don big white pearls as the perfect foil for tanned chests and tight white jeans. The event, which drew 2,500 guests, is the 1996 White Party at the Vizcaya Museum and Gardens in Miami. Founded in 1984, this annual event was referred to in *The New York Times* as "the crown jewel in the international list of dance-until-after-dawn events called circuit parties" staged primarily as fund-raisers for AIDS charities.

OPPOSITE: Photographer Harry Benson is adept at catching the in-between moment that reveals his subject. For this photo of Daryl Hannah, an unpacked box containing a tangle of pearls and the dirty floors of her new Manhattan apartment conspired to create the image of an all-too-earthbound angel. Benson remembers spying the pearls in a half-opened box and asking Hannah if she could "do something" with them. "Being an actress, she wrapped them around herself," he says. "Pearls do instantly give a woman a lift," continues the Scottish-born photojournalist— even if she is just wearing a blanket.

The efforts of many scientists contributed to the development of today's streamlined pearl-culturing technique. Three Japanese researchers—a biologist named Tokichi Nishikawa; Tatsuhei Mise, a carpenter; and Kokichi Mikimoto, the son of a noodle maker—all developed techniques for the cultivation of much-sought-after round pearls. But it was Mr. Mikimoto's persistence and sophisticated vision that turned practical research into a billion-dollar industry. He and his wife founded pearl farms in Ago Bay and cultured their first blister pearl in 1893; Mr. Mikimoto received a patent for the process in 1896. In the aftermath of a red tide epidemic in 1904 that destroyed all 850,000 of his oysters, while combing through each of the dead mollusks, Mr. Mikimoto discovered their legacy. Before they perished, some of his oysters had produced his first glistening crop of round cultured pearls. Eventually he bought from his competitors the rights to use improved culturing techniques and further refined the process of pearl culturing that is still used today: a round sphere of shell from mussels imported

𝒫earls against the skin heighten the
eroticism of this anonymous photograph.
"There was a tradition of a certain kind of
semi-illicit, under-the-counter photo of nudes
which were obviously made to titillate,"
says Philippe Garner, a senior director of
Sotheby's, London, and current owner of this
photo. "Visitors to Paris might venture into
the red-light district and take home a
photograph like this."
OPPOSITE: Henry Cyril Paget, the extravagant
and eccentric 5th Marquis of Anglesey,
known as the "Dancing Marquis." Paget
punctuates his costume for an early 1900s
production of *The Runaway Boy* with some of
his extensive collection of jewelry, including
a thigh-grazing rope of sizable pearls.

from the United States is surgically inserted along with a
small piece of mantle tissue (the thick skin that protects the
oyster's body inside the shell and produces the secretions
that form the mother-of-pearl lining of the shell, and the
pearl itself) from the body of another oyster.

It was Mr. Mikimoto's sales and marketing savvy
that changed the course of history in the jewelry business.
At a time when most businesses stayed within their own
territory, Mr. Mikimoto was one of the early global thinkers.
By 1921, from his well-established shop in Tokyo—the first
store to specialize in selling pearls—K. Mikimoto and Company began selling the new round cultured pearls around
the world. He then added branch stores and liaison outlets
in major capitals, including London, Paris, New York,
Chicago, Los Angeles, San Francisco, Shanghai, and Bombay. With his eye on a future where every woman in the
world would wear cultured pearls, Mr. Mikimoto employed
dramatic vehicles to call attention to his new pearl product.
For the 1939 World's Fair in New York, he created a Liberty
Bell of pearls, and in 1952 Mikimoto staged a nationwide
tour of a dress, handbag, and jewelry made of 100,000 cultured pearls. He enticed some of the newsmakers of the
day to wear his cultured pearls by giving them away. One
by one, his detractors capitulated and the "Pearl King," as
he was called, finally convinced naysayers—from the most
prestigious jewelers to stubborn connoisseurs—that cultured pearls should be accepted for their authenticity as a
new category of pearls. Not imitations, but real pearls. He
wanted every woman in the world to wear Japanese pearls.

Under Mr. Mikimoto's aggressive leadership, the
Japanese controlled the international cultured pearl market for the next thirty years. Even today, countries like Australia, Tahiti, Myanmar (formerly Burma), and China
employ Japanese assistance in their culturing technique,
Japanese technicians, and Japanese distribution channels.

$\mathcal{H}$er real name was Alice Prin, and during the six years that she lived with and modeled for photographer Man Ray, they pushed the creative limits of photography during the Surrealist movement. Kiki de Montparnasse, as she was known, was as photogenic in a hat and pearls as she was in the nude.

RIGHT: Love at first sight: Baron Leo d'Erlanger first saw Edwina, an actress, model, and dancer from New Mexico, in a London train station, and according to legend, fell in love on the spot. Her revealingly sandaled feet apparently stirred his particular passion. D'Erlanger traced her across the ocean, and the two were married in 1929. This Cecil Beaton portrait appeared in the June 1949 issue of *Vogue* and illustrates her ability to play an amusing hat against classically beautiful fashion and pearls. Married for over 50 years, the couple spent much of their time at Star of Venus, their Tunisian palace, filled with treasures, including 150-year-old mother-of-pearl cabinets from the Ottoman Empire.

Elizabeth Taylor's daughter, Liza Todd, gave these X-shaped baroque earrings to her mother as a Christmas present and snapped the picture for the designer, Christopher Walling.

OPPOSITE: For *Girl with a Pearl Earring*, Jan Vermeer used a scumble, or thin layerering of off-white paint, over the brown shadow of the model's neck to define the pearl earring. The more opaque white at the bottom of the pearl reflects her white collar. An expert at painting pearls, Vermeer would always blend the white of the pearl with the underlying skin tone to highlight the intimate and reflective quality of this lustrous gem.

The Japanese directly produce, help produce, and market 75 percent of all the cultured pearls in the world and spearhead a $5 billion cultivated pearl industry.

Regardless of whether they are natural or cultured, pearls are generally classified by their origins in fresh water or salt water. Freshwater pearls develop inside mussels that are found in rivers and streams throughout the world. The most well recognized are the Biwa variety from Japan; the most prolific sources are located in China. For example, in 1998 China produced 700 tons of freshwater and saltwater pearls, about 10 percent of which were of a quality high enough (with regard to color, luster, shape, size, and surface) to use in jewelry. That same year, the Chinese produced a historic first crop of round freshwater pearls that were 15 mm in diameter. Freshwater pearls are cultured by inserting a tiny piece of mantle tissue (the oyster's natural internal blanket protection) from freshwater mussels. This mantle-only process produces a pearl of pure nacre, like those increasingly rare natural seawater pearls.

Natural saltwater pearls are born of the *Pinctada radiata* oyster in the Persian Gulf and the Red Sea. Owing to pollution and overfishing, natural pearls have become rare. Today, only about one-half of one percent of all the pearls in the world are

natural. Most of those available are purchased by private collectors and never reach the marketplace. In effect, pearls suitable for fine jewelry have always been rare. Even when the quest for pearls reached its peak during the Renaissance, and pearls were plentiful, demand overrode the supply. Before pearls were cultured, only one oyster in ten to twenty thousand contained a usable pearl. Some divers could spend a lifetime and never find enough matching pearls to make a necklace.

By the 1920s natural pearls were so scarce that it took one of the most discriminating New York designers, Raymond C. Yard (the preeminent society jeweler established in 1922), ten years to assemble the uniformly shaped and colored natural pearls needed for a necklace John D. Rockefeller purchased in 1929 for his wife. The single-strand necklace, which was sold at auction by Sotheby's in Geneva in 1998, was actually derived from a more elaborate two-strand necklace with diamond and pearl finials (rigid sections) made originally for Martha Baird Rockefeller in the 1950s. A necklace of this sort, with sixty-three perfectly matched pearls ranging in size from 6.80 mm to 11.15 mm, might be impossible to duplicate today. Natural pearls that are traded today and sold at auction are for the most part recycled pearls from the past.

For both saltwater and freshwater pearls, it is the quality of the pearl that determines its worth. The thickness of the nacre affects the beauty and ultimate desirability. The more luminescent the pearl, the more perfectly aligned the layers of nacre. The colorful orient, or rainbow effect, on the surface of a pearl indicates the refraction of light among the microscopic crystals within the layers of nacre. The satiny finish of some South Sea pearls is a result of the increased spacing between the layers of nacre

---

An art collector, world traveler, and a regular in the Boston social columns, Isabella Stewart Gardner was alternately slandered and praised for her individuality.

In 1894 society portraitist Anders Zorn captured a 54-year-old "Belle" enthusiastically calling friends onto the terrace to watch fireworks light up the Venice night. Mrs. Gardner's verve is certainly accentuated by her famous long strand of pearls with a 98-carat pear-shaped ruby pendant from Boucheron.

"She wore jewelry in very dramatic ways," says Susan Sinclair, archivist at the Isabella Stewart Gardner Museum in Boston. "In public, she was very chic."

The first of the pearls Belle Gardner would become so well known for was bought by her husband, Jack, in 1874 at London's Hancock & Co. A single strand of 44 pearls with a diamond clasp, it cost $4,500.

Starting in 1884, she bought pearls from Boucheron during her biannual trips to Paris, and eventually her necklace swelled to contain 231 pearls—long enough to encircle her neck many times and still drop to her knees. She wore her pearls during an audience with Pope Leo XIII, and it is said that he took the long rope in his hands as she knelt before him.

In the years prior to her death in 1924, this rope was broken up into seven necklaces that were gifted to her nieces, granddaughters, and the wives of her nephews.

caused by warmer waters. Being able to see your face reflected in the lustrous surface of a pearl is a good indicator of quality.

Along with color, luster, size, and surface, shape determines a pearl's appeal and value. Some of the most recognizable shapes range from tiny seed or raisin-like specimens to the smooth giant South Sea baubles so fashionable with the international set in the United States and Europe. Perfectly round spheres are prized for traditional necklaces of one or more strands. The more round, the more valuable, and today the larger and rounder, the more alluring.

Most pearls, however, are irregular in shape and are known as baroque pearls. These textured pearls come in a range of shapes, from the simple off-round sphere to symmetrical baroque shapes, known as teardrops or pear shapes, and more complex versions resembling flower petals, wings, bridges, and butterflies. Some baroque pearls are joined together as twin or triplet shapes.

The different sizes and shapes are the result of where the pearl grows inside the oyster, the size and shape of the nucleus (in the case of cultured pearls), and how long the pearl has been allowed to mature. It takes two to three years to make a fine-quality cultured pearl, although most are produced in eight months to two years.

Round, off-round, symmetrical, or baroque, where do all these pearls go? Seventy percent of all gem-quality pearls are used for necklaces, the 16- to 18-inch single strand being the most popular. "We call this single-strand necklace the beginning of a woman's jewelry wardrobe," says John Loring, design director at Tiffany & Co. The average price for a 16- to 18-inch choker of medium to better quality 6.5 mm to 7 mm round Japanese Akoya pearls (named after the typical Japanese Akoya oyster used for producing the country's cultured pearls) is $1,500.

Since the death of her husband, Prince Johannes, Gloria von Thurn und Taxis has managed to hold on to the family fortune. Although she sold over two million dollars' worth of magnificent pearl jewelry at auction in 1992, she did not sell all of it. The beautiful princess adores pearls, whether they are her black ones or the magnificent strand of South Sea pearls she wears here in Robert Mapplethorpe's stunning image.

Ten other styles represent the basic repertoire of pearl necklaces. A *bib* necklace has more than three strands. The collar, whose name is derived from a dog collar, contains multiple strands of pearls that fit closely around the neck. While a *choker* was traditionally 14 to 16 inches long and a *princess* necklace 17 to 18 inches, both are called chokers today. A *matinée*-length necklace is 20 to 24 inches long. *Opera*-length necklaces range from 30 to 36 inches in length. *Ropes* are necklaces longer than 36 inches. A *sautoir* is a rope, as is a *lariat*. A *torsade* is a number of strands twisted to form a choker or one of the longer lengths.

In addition to their role in history, pearls have other uses. Some pearls are used for medicinal purposes. Beginning at twenty years of age, the founder of the modern pearl industry, Mr. Mikimoto, consumed two pearls for breakfast every day in his belief that pearls increased longevity. He died in 1954 at ninety-six. Pearl remedies have been used to treat every imaginable physical ailment, including heart disease, jaundice, eczema, indigestion, insomnia, gynecological problems, measles, whooping cough, cataracts and other eye ailments, ear problems, headaches, ulcers, gout, smallpox, lung diseases, and even madness and leprosy. Today Chinese, Japanese, Indian, and some European cultures remain committed to their belief in the healing and rejuvenating qualities of pearls. Crushed pearls are used in cosmetics and consumed as a source of calcium, energy, and vitality.

Pearls might have mystical, mythical, and medicinal powers, but in combination with their natural ability to adorn the human body, it is their natural scarcity that keeps the allure alive. The demand for pearls is so great, particularly in America, that the supply of natural and cultured pearls cannot meet it. Copies abound. The widely recognized Majorica brand pearls, for example, are made by dipping glass beads into a coating made of especially iridescent North Atlantic fish scales.

The Venetians developed faux pearls in the sixteenth century by blowing bubbles of iridescent glass and filling the bubbles with wax. By the seventeenth century a French rosary maker named Jacquin developed *essence d'orient,* a compound of fish scale liquid and varnish. Coating the inside of glass beads with this iridescent solution, then filling the beads with wax, the Parisian outdid the Venetians and created a better quality faux pearl. Jacquin's method is still used today and is the basis of the Majorica™ method.

Another technique used to manufacture imitation pearls is to build a sturdy layer of iridescence on the outside of a bead by dipping solid glass or plastic balls into the *essence d'orient*. The number of layers determines the quality and price of the final product.

Fake, faux, costume, imitation, or simulated, these pearls never saw the inside of an oyster. They are pretenders, a concept understood and practiced by the Chinese as early as the first century. While sometimes more expensive than the cheapest all-nacre variety, imitation pearl jewelry is a fashion standby for women who don't have a great deal of money to spend on jewelry.

Perennial fashion editrix Carrie Donovan has been commenting on and setting trends since her days at *Vogue*, *Harper's Bazaar*, and *The New York Times*.

"I've always been insane about pearls," says Ms. Donovan. "They don't have to be real." Over the years Carrie has owned many strands of fine faux pearls, along with other pearl accessories. The woman, who may be more familiar to a younger generation as a spokeswoman for the chain of Old Navy sportswear stores, now favors Carolee Designs (an American brand of costume pearls). "First of all, they are so well priced, and they are beautiful," says Donovan. "Unless you are really a pearl expert, you can't tell the difference."

Like her personality—and her glasses—Carrie's pearls are oversized, impossible to ignore. "I have large features and a long face. I like the statement of the big pearl. Little ones look too dinky. I love them. And what is so marvelous is that when they look old and crummy, I go out and buy a new strand."

*A*s earthly metaphors for purity and inno-cence, these luminescent gems are the natural representatives for those milestones in our early lives. Some of the turning points for which we offer pearls as a celebratory gift include birth, baptism, first communion, confirmation, bat mitzvah, sweet sixteenth birthday, high school graduation, twenty-first birthday, college graduation, engagement to be married, and betrothal. Perhaps pearls are a girl's best friend, after all. At least her first ones, forming a bond that lasts a lifetime. Pearls are often a young girl's first everlasting gift; one, unlike a rattle or a sterling porringer, that grows with her. Pearls' aqueous origins offer a logical association with cleansings, with occasions that are about

NOCENTS

new beginnings in life. A newborn baby wears a tiny pearl bracelet, a baby girl's ears are pierced with pearls when she is a day or two old. Some young girls accessorize their first party dresses with a string of delicate pearls, while others receive a pearl or more each birthday so that as they reach maturity they have their first pearl necklace.

Every heir to the Russian czarist throne until Alexei—when Nicholas II gave it to the state fund—used a gold rattle encrusted with pearls, emeralds, rubies, diamonds, coral, and ivory; pearls, however, are usually associated with girls. The etymology of the classic girl's name Margaret may have its roots in an ancient word for the pearl. Some linguists and historians define Margaret or Margarita as a derivation of *murwari*, Persian for "child of the sea," or "child of light." Is it accident or chance that it is also the name of a pearl-bearing oyster—*Margaritifera vulgaris*—an island off the once pearl-rich coast of Venezuela, the heroine of Goethe's *Faust,* and saints? According to George Frederick Kunz in *The Book of the Pearl,* Sainte Margaret of Antioch was the virgin martyr, "who, before the fifth century [A.D.], was the embodiment of feminine innocence and faith overcoming evil, and who is often represented wearing a string of pearls." Margherita, the dowager queen of Italy, had so many strands of

PAGE 20: *Grand* Duchess Anastasia, daughter of Czar Nicholas of Russia and his wife, Alexandra.
RIGHT: **In 1987 Sally Mann photographed her five-year-old daughter Jessica playing dress-up in her mother's sixteen-inch necklace of 13-12 mm white South Sea pearls.**

The four daughters of Czar Nicholas II and Alexandra (left to right): Maria, Tatiana, Anastasia, and Olga. Five years after this portrait was made, the whole family was captured and executed by members of the Bolshevik Party in a town called Yekaterinburg, putting a bloody end to the Romanov dynasty and a shocking punctuation mark in the Russian Revolution.

When they were being buried, about 18 pounds of diamonds were found hidden in the clothing of the empress and her daughters, and the empress had several pearl necklaces sewn into the waist of her dress. Naturally, all the diamonds and pearls were seized, and in the mid-1920s much of the Romanovs' jewelry was sold to raise money.

pearls that they started just under her chin and reached down to her knees. Her husband, King Umberto, lived up to his promise to add for her every birthday one magnificent rope of pearls to the necklace she inherited as queen. Margherita ended up with one of the finest collections of pearls in Europe.

Hindu legend holds that Krishna the Adorable, the eighth incarnation of the great god Vishnu and the favorite Hindu god, discovered the pearl when he drew it from the depths of the sea as a gift for his daughter on her wedding day. And the Indians also believed that when God created the world, each of the four elements offered a gift. Air bestowed a rainbow to serve as God's halo; fire provided the light of a meteor; earth offered a ruby to adorn his forehead; and water created a pearl to comfort his heart.

The first milestone of youth and innocence is the formal acknowledgment of birth itself, in the form of a baptism. "Baptism is a blessing in recognition of the child's entrance into this world, regardless of the divinity to whom he or she will give thanks or ask for protection," says the Reverend Stephen Smith, whose ministerial, addiction-recovery, and coaching duties have taken him to three continents. "This initiation service, characterized by immersion in or anointment with water, recognizes the child's inability to fend for himself or herself and asks for the spirit's sanctification. A gift is a concrete symbol of one's honor or esteem for the dignitary. It is my opinion that, from first recorded history when the wise men from the East bore gifts to the child that these shamans interpreted to be the King of the Jews, that tradition of giving gifts at the birth of a child has perpetuated in Western culture ever since and wherever Christianity has spread."

The former White House chief of staff for Jacqueline Kennedy, Letitia Baldrige, discusses the custom of gift-giving in her update of *The Amy Vanderbilt Complete Book of Etiquette*. She suggests a baby pin of antique seed pearls as a christening or baby present. "A baby can't appreciate a piece of jewelry," Baldrige writes, "but a four-year-old girl looks forward to every birthday party and special occasion when she will be allowed to wear 'her very own . . . jewelry.'" As a child, the present Queen Mother of England received a necklace of small pearls from her family and reveled in wearing them, alternating them enthusiastically with her string of coral beads. She later strung the beads into a necklace of coral and pearls for each of her young daughters.

The four daughters of Russia's last czar, Nicholas II, and his beloved empress, Alexandra (whose favorite jewel was the pearl), appear to have worn pearls from birth. Early portraits show Olga, Tatiana, Maria, and Anastasia wearing matching white dresses and, as toddlers, delicate little pearl necklaces and graduating to larger pearl chokers as young girls, again wearing matching dresses. "Their parents set aside two pearls (perfect spheres of about 8 mm each) every year for each of the girls so that on their sixteenth birthdays they each had a collar of thirty-two pearls," says Nick Nicholson, who curated the exhibit "Jewels of the Romanovs" that toured the United States from 1996 to 1998. "I'm sure that their parents would have kept doing this until the girls were married, so that they would have fabulous tea-length necklaces of flawless creamy white pearls."

Since 1914 thousands of girls across the United States have begun assembling their first pearl necklaces at birth with something called Add-a-Pearl. (The name is a registered trademark of the Juergens and Anderson Company in Chicago.) Through jewelers, families purchase the necklaces one pearl at a time. They start with the fine gold chain and from one to five pearls, adding more for birthdays and special occasions so that by the time a child reaches the ages of eighteen to twenty, she has a fifteen-inch necklace with anywhere from 133 to 167 pearls, depending on the size of the pearls.

Charlotte Ford, daughter of Henry Ford II, fondly remembers her Add-a-Pearls. "Pearls were one of the first presents I got. It's a great idea for kids. Mine were in one long strand that could be made into two." Letitia Baldrige, America's premier etiquette expert, also shares the sentiment. "My memory of Add-a-Pearls goes back to when I was two or three. They were my first pearls," she says. "My mother, grandmothers, and my aunts would all give

Pearls are a family tradition that was passed on to Ruth Elizabeth Brodie, shown here in her Bryn Mawr graduation portrait from 1935, by her mother, Caroline Buchanan Brodie, who wore pearls throughout her life. Ruth wanted her mother's multistrand necklace, but as often happens, the pearls vanished from her mother's household without a trace.
OPPOSITE: **In 1915 Barbara Hutton was a healthy three-year-old in a hat and pearls.**

them to me. Each time, the little gold chain would go back to the jeweler and the new pearls would be strung on it. They were so sweet, I just loved them. When I was about nine, I grew too big for them, really. It was time to switch to a much larger necklace."

"We had the same thing in France," says New York decorator Robert Couturier. "I think that every girl was given pearls. Each year, they would be given four or five more pearls. By the time they were eighteen, they had one whole string of pearls around their necks."

"Every year, my grandmother gave me a pearl for my birthday and a pearl for Christmas," says Lady Sarah Churchill, granddaugher of Consuelo Vanderbilt, the first American to marry a titled Englishman, the duke of Marlborough. "They were kept at a jeweler in the Burlington Arcade in London. As I got older, sometimes I got five or six at a time, and the pearls got bigger. I ended up with nearly two strings. I bought one more row myself, the short row, to make it three."

"I think it's a lovely thing to start with your children when they are little—in our days it was," says the Dowager Viscountess Lady Weir. "My grandmother must have given me the pearls. By the time I was sixteen or seventeen, I had not a large necklace, but a really nice necklace of medium-sized pearls that a young girl could wear—a nice, single strand, down to about my chest. I did the same with my children, grandchildren, and great-grandchildren." As a footnote to the tradition of passing pearls through the family, especially in honor of the milestones of youth, Lady Weir notes that her stepdaughter in Scotland "has a tiara of pearls from her Scottish mother which she wore when she was married."

As young women leave their childhoods behind, historically societies have embraced some sort of coming-of-age ritual to invite courtship and marriage. In Western society it has been the *debut,* derived from a French expression meaning "go for the goal" or, less euphemistically, "go for the husband." The ritual was begun by the English at formal presentation "courts," or grand balls, during which English aristocrats' daughters were introduced to society by making a ceremonious curtsy to the queen. Pocahontas was the first American debutante, when in 1616 she was presented to the court of James I, as the wife of the English gentleman John Rolfe. Some other Americans who also took their British bows have included sisters Rosemary and Kathleen Kennedy, Pamela Digby (Churchill Hayward Harriman), Consuelo

Elizabeth Taylor starred with her real-life friend Montgomery Clift in George Stevens's Academy Award—winning film *A Place in the Sun* in 1951. Her pearls are a metaphor for her youth and innocence.

Vanderbilt, Doris Duke, and Barbara Hutton. The system began to relax after World War II, and in 1958 Queen Elizabeth II, in a clean sweep of formal court customs, abandoned the debut.

In the United States a debutante was originally presented to society at a tea in her home, followed by a dinner and dancing for family and friends. The intimate celebrations grew more lavish in the 1930s, culminating in such opulent debuts as Barbara Hutton's $60,000 (more than a half million dollars today) supper dance for a thousand guests at the Ritz-Carlton Hotel in 1930 and Charlotte Ford's $250,000 blow-out at the Detroit Country Club in 1959, also for a thousand guests.

As debutantes continue to dance the night away at the Junior League and Infirmary balls in New York City and their old-line equivalents around the country, their long white dresses, over-the-elbow-length white gloves, and pearls are *de rigueur*.

"I got my very first pearls from my grandmother when I was confirmed," says Sidney Biddle Barrows, whose prominent American family dates back to the *Mayflower* and who caused a social scandal when she was exposed and indicted in 1984 as the captain of a very elite escort service. "My grandmother gave me a gold cross with a single line of small round pearls. When my niece was confirmed, I gave it to her. And all of my bridesmaids wore single-strand pearl necklaces and pearl stud

An Edie Sedgwick prototype, the notorious Brenda Frazier was a debutante with flair, commanding as much newspaper copy as movie stars of the day—Burelles news-clipping agency found 5,000 mentions of her in one six-month period. Her debutante ball held at the Ritz cost $75,000 in 1938, and was infiltrated by *The New York Daily News* photographers posing as guests in evening dress. A picture of Brenda in her trendsetting pink strapless gown and a pearl-and-diamond necklace was featured on the November 14 cover of *Life*. Brenda was so well known that letters addressed "Brenda Frazier, The World's Prettiest Debutante," or merely with her picture pasted on the envelope, would find their way to her door. Brenda was among the "Glamour Girls" straddling fame and the upper echelons of society. Later, she developed a serious addiction to prescription drugs and had a nervous breakdown in 1954. For one of her last appearances, a lecture at Westover (her alma mater), Ms. Frazier clung to her ritual toilette and would not leave home without her pearls.

Here she is with her daughter, Brenda Victoria, during happier times at the Stork Club in 1950. Like mother, like daughter: both adopt pearls as part of their persona.

OPPOSITE: Be-pearled and blindfolded guests enjoying wedding festivities in Biarritz.

earrings," continues the matter-of-fact Barrows, who currently lectures and writes books. "Everybody had her own necklace, and everyone had a pair of pearl stud earrings. Actually, I can't imagine there's anyone in the world who doesn't have them."

While Ms. Barrows's story might include a risqué approach to business, her youth with pearls is as traditional as her familial roots. "A girl's whole life unfolds between two veils—the communicant's and the bride's," wrote the Comtesse de Gence in 1910, in her discussion of the similarities between first communion and marriage practices, including the solemn ceremonies performed before an audience, the white dresses, and the presence of pearls. Just as a young girl might wear or receive pearls for her official entry into the church, so might a young woman wear or receive pearls for her wedding.

The purity associated with pearls is reflected in their historical abundance around weddings—from engagement rings and ornamental jewelry to embroidery on gowns, caps, veils, or even shoes. The Greeks considered pearls the official wedding gem and believed that they would safeguard marital happiness. Just as many a maiden sent her soldier off to the Crusades with a pearl for protection, many a gallant knight brought his true love a pearl from the East for her wedding day. In an ancient Indian Hindu text the word *krisana* meant "pearl." That text, almost three thousand years old, contains the story of Krishna, "the preserver," who discovered and brought forth pearls from the depths of the sea to give to his daughter Pandaïa on her wedding day. While we might not cover ourselves with pearls as the bride, groom, and male and female guests did in Elizabethan England or seventeenth-century France, we still associate pearls with weddings.

Monday is the day of the pearl and represents the day of wealth if you get married on Monday. The month of June earned its reputation as a propitious month for marriage because it was the month in which Juno, the Roman queen of the heavens and goddess of femininity and fertility (both mystical attributes of the pearl), was married. Depending on the source, pearls are the traditional gift for a couple's twelfth or thirtieth anniversary.

While weddings themselves have not changed much, the process of selection and announcement has altered. The custom of betrothal, or the intention and commitment to marry, has persisted in the streamlined form of the engagement. Historically, betrothals were business arrangements which were sealed with a financial exchange and sanctified in a church ceremony. In ancient Rome they were contracts between the elders. During the Middle Ages betrothals were often arranged between families when their children were infants, and thus were great political, military, and monetary alliances forged. Among some tribes in the Australian outback marriages have been prearranged for unborn grandchildren. In Islamic and Eastern cultures parents traditionally arranged the betrothals, and the parents of the prospective groom were required to make the initial contact. It was during the Middle Ages that marriage announcements were usually celebrated with the gift of an engagement ring to demonstrate the man's commitment to the future wedding date.

Until the early twentieth century the pearl was the ultimate gem for an engagement ring. Barbara Hutton's first engagement ring was a black pearl (which her husband, Prince Alexis Midvani, acquired with the money he received as a divorce settlement from his first wife, Louise Van Alen); the last empress of Russia's was a pink pearl, and since 1940 the Queen Mother, whose signature jewel is the pearl, has worn a single pearl, surrounded by diamonds, as her engagement ring. In the 1980s D. D. Ryan, a New York socialite and part of fashion designer Halston's entourage, lost a pearl from her engagement ring at Studio 54, the infamous disco on West 54th Street in Manhattan. According to her friend, jewelry designer Kenneth Jay Lane, it was "a beautiful

In the 1920s it was popular, or "a matter of necessity," according to one former flapper, for a lady to tuck her handkerchief into her bracelet for the evening. In 1929 Diane Goldman slipped hers under a wristful of pearls. Fond of pearls, the young New Yorker also wore a bandeau of pearls in her hair.

A year later, when she married Sam Avirom, Diane accessorized her white satin wedding dress with more pearls. When their formal wedding portrait arrived from the photographer, surprisingly, her dress had been hand-tinted blue, but the couple loved the photo and kept it.

*W*ith her poodle, Countess Court Haugwitz-Reventlow, the former Barbara Hutton, watches a tennis match at the Everglades Club in Palm Beach. Her penchant for the simplicity of pearls is shown here in her pearl earrings and drop-pearl bracelet. Toward the end of her life Barbara kept her jewelry in three modified briefcases beside her bed and never took off her pearl necklace, Pasha diamond ring, smaller pearl and diamond ring, and gold armbands.

OPPOSITE: Count and Countess Haugwitz-Reventlow are seen socializing during the finals at Wimbledon in 1937. Hutton is wearing the pearl necklace, a gift from her father, that had once belonged to Marie Antoinette. From Empress Eugénie's ruby tiara and Countess de Castiglione's emeralds to the black pearl engagement ring that her first husband, Prince Alexis Mdivani bought her, Barbara's jewelry was legendary.

Van Cleef ring and a great big pearl. They found it when they were sweeping up the next day and returned it to her. Do you believe that? It's amazing."

In the sixteenth century the wedding ring was declared an essential element of the marriage sacrament by the Council of Trent. The Egyptian pharaohs wore their wedding rings on the third finger of the left hand because they believed that a vein, called the *vena amoris,* ran from that finger directly to the heart. Since the heart controlled both life and love, this finger was the most honored, the most deserving of the pledge of love. The Romans believed that the fourth finger was protected because it cannot be raised without the company of the neighboring finger, and that the left hand was more secure because it was used less often. In the early Christian church the fourth finger symbolized the earthly love of man for woman, their marriage together, and the hope of Heaven to follow. After the groom said "With this ring, I thee wed," he held the ring over the tip of the thumb, saying "In the name of the Father"; then over the second finger, saying "and of the Son"; then on the tip of the third finger, saying "and of the Holy Ghost." Slipping it on the fourth finger, he said "Amen."

Since she admittedly forced her daughter, Consuelo, to marry the duke of Marlborough in order to add a title to the Vanderbilt legacy, Alva Vanderbilt gave her daughter as a wedding present the illustrious pearl necklace that had belonged to Catherine the Great. According to Stuart E. Jacobson and Jill Spalding in their book about gift giving, *Only the Best,* Consuelo's father "William was less eager for his daughter's unhappiness, [so] he came through with a diamond tiara for Consuelo, two and a half million dollars' worth of railroad stock for the duke, and a hundred-thousand-dollar annual allowance for each."

American heiress Anna Gould, daughter of railroad baron Jay Gould, picked her own royal titles, becoming a countess when she married Paul Ernest Boniface de Castellane, a financially fragile but legitimate French count. While the family disapproved of the Boni's obvious bounty hunting, Ms. Gould's wedding booty included a diamond coronet, a rope of two hundred diamonds, and a necklace of eight hundred pearls. The second time around, the second-generation Gould heiress married the duc de Talleyrand-Périgord, who was actually her first husband's cousin.

Sometimes wedding pearls are good imitations. "For a family in Montreal, one of the sisters was wearing a full pearl choker of mine," says Kenneth Jay Lane, whose signature pearl necklaces are the often alabaster fakes coveted by women around the world, from Princess Diana to Jacqueline Kennedy Onassis. However, he continues, "As the bride was walking down the aisle, it broke."

Pearls have been the jewelry of choice for official milestone photographs of young women through the years, especially those who have been clients of New York's venerable Bachrach Studio, such as Amanda Burden, New Jersey governor Christine Todd Whitman, and the young Jacqueline Bouvier. "Our clients usually bring their own pearls that have been handed down through the family," says Pauline Nielsen, former manager at Bachrach in New York. "We suggest they bring pearls anyway. We believe that, for anyone, a black dress and a string of pearls is still the ultimate in elegance.

      "Everyone has a story about her pearls," continues Nielsen. "The women talk about how their grandmothers wore the pearls on their wedding days and how they plan to wear them too; or that their

Tina Barney captured this photo of her niece Polly wearing pearls as she prepares to take her wedding vows in May 1998. Even today this quintessentially pure gem, here used as fringe on a choker, is still a favorite among young brides.

pearls are from a wonderful vacation in Cancún; and how their mothers and grandmother wore the same ones for their portraits. The sentimental attachment is worth more than money. My own mother has a set of freshwater pearls. She had never had any before, and my father purchased the necklace for her on their twenty-fifth wedding anniversary. She wears them on every special occasion. Mother has other jewelry that is more valuable, but her pearls are more valuable in sentiment."

"Pearls are the only thing I recommend," says Christina Krupka, the second-generation head of D'Arlene Studios in New York City, the official photographers for the Junior League debutante ball and creators of other rite-of-passage portraits. "The shape of a pearl is timeless. Pearls are in good taste without being ostentatious." The photographer also points out, with as much pride as irony: "We still use the same drape across the shoulders and tied in the back that was used for my own high school picture." However, some things have changed. Engagement photos now often include the groom. The couple arrives at the studio in business attire. It is not unusual for the woman to bring her mother's or grandmother's pearls. The full-length wedding portrait has fallen out of favor. "Very few women come in with a bridal gown anymore. Today the photos are mostly color shots from the wedding. Women are older now. They are often working. And they don't have Mom helping them. For the fall season, 1997, I did three full-length newspaper portraits. One was for the wife of an Englishman whose heritage could be traced back to the father of Anne Boleyn. While the bride wore diamonds at her wedding, she wore pearls for her engagement photograph. Interestingly, the other two young women did come with their wedding gowns, their pearls . . . and their mothers."

After their wedding in May 1964, E.T. and Lyn Williams, an alum of the Me-De-So Cotillion in Baltimore, headed closer to their shared stomping grounds in the North, to build their lives in New York and Sag Harbor.

LORDS

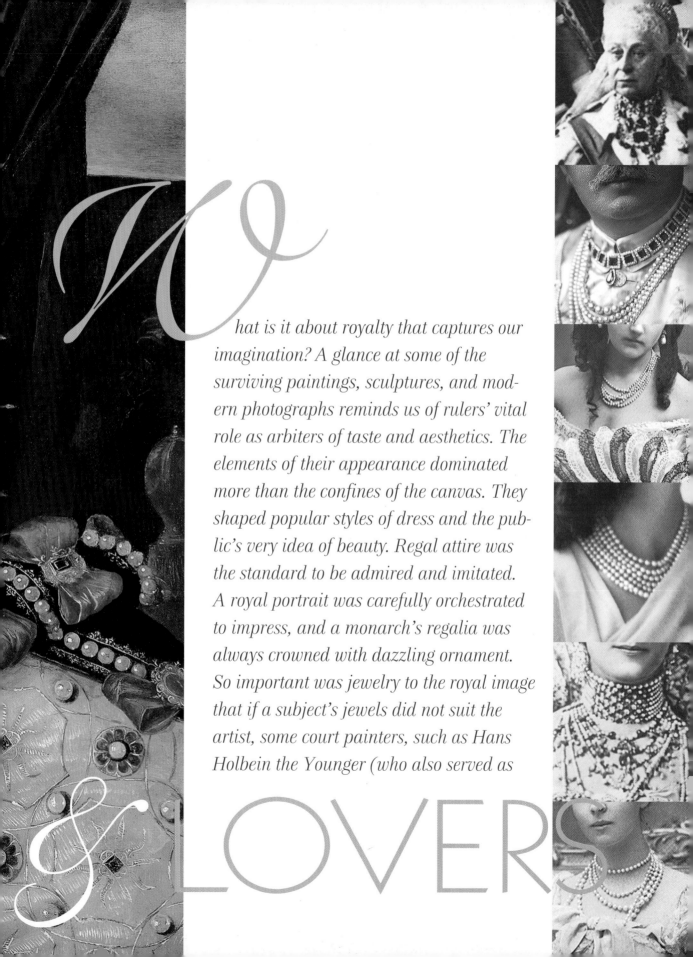

W

O

hat is it about royalty that captures our imagination? A glance at some of the surviving paintings, sculptures, and modern photographs reminds us of rulers' vital role as arbiters of taste and aesthetics. The elements of their appearance dominated more than the confines of the canvas. They shaped popular styles of dress and the public's very idea of beauty. Regal attire was the standard to be admired and imitated. A royal portrait was carefully orchestrated to impress, and a monarch's regalia was always crowned with dazzling ornament. So important was jewelry to the royal image that if a subject's jewels did not suit the artist, some court painters, such as Hans Holbein the Younger (who also served as

& LOVERS

a jeweler to England's Henry VIII), would employ a bit of artistic license and embellish the jewelry to fit their version of the public's expectation of how a ruler should appear.

The alliance of pearls with divine power was not lost on centuries of sovereigns. The crown itself, one of the earliest and most representative symbols of royalty, forms a constellation around the head, which suggests the heavenly authority. In the first century B.C. Julius Caesar's pearl diadem, or the double circlets of pearls worn by his general and triumvirate officer, Pompey, bear witness to both the pearl's ability to communicate the divine status of ancient rulers and the early male leaders' enjoyment of pearls as jewels. In the eighth century France's King Pépin the Short created a prototype for the modern crown when he set a gold circlet with pearls. Another early example of this divine association is the famous sixth-century mosaic at San Vitale in Ravenna, Italy. The tiles depict Emperor Justinian in his pearl-embroidered cap, beside his wife, Theodora, whose grand pearl-encircled tiara drips with strings of pearls, suspended from each side, which descend over the pearl-encrusted shoulders of her robe and well beyond her heart. The pair appear as almighty beings holding forth among the members of their court.

For the privileged elite of the Renaissance, pearls possessed both a rare beauty and a more subtle, practical quality: their natural luminescence functioned as personal stage lighting in the dark interiors of palaces and castles. Imagine the ethereal impact of candlelight and pearls. Pearls become the ultimate makeup that enhances the deeply feminine complexion of the woman who is wearing them, and they flatter the strongest features of the man who dons them.

The right to amass pearls at any cost and the covetous display of these lustrous gems were considered as much the divine right of rulers as was their right to rule. Over the centuries leaders may have accumulated more diamonds and other colorful gems, even more buildings and territory, but the road to ornament as status symbol always leads back to the pearl. It is perfect. Without polishing, piercing, or planing, pearls can be woven together, strung side by side or placed in individual settings. Pearls stand on their own with exquisite splendor, and their distinctive white coloring and special luminescence complement multijeweled designs. Their composition uniquely catches light, and before the advent of cut gems, they illuminated the unfaceted stones of

Princess Marie-Chantal of Greece, formerly Marie-Chantal Miller, of the duty-free Robert Miller family. The Miller women are known for their penchant for South Sea pearls, like the ones Marie-Chantal uses to light her face and both wrists in this portrait by David Seidner.

antiquity. Later, after techniques to facet gems were developed in about A.D. 1450, their subtle beauty and dignity tempered their showier counterparts, such as diamonds, emeralds, and rubies. The pearl possesses a beauty that, in any culture, country, or century, everyone understands.

Pearls have survived in their regal role for more than six millennia. The oldest known surviving necklace was found in 1901 in present-day Iran, among the ruins of the winter palace of Persian kings. The necklace, composed of three ropes of seventy-two pearls and gold disks and believed to be prayer beads ensuring fertility and long life in the next world, now resides in the Louvre Museum in Paris. It belonged to a Persian princess and dates back to the Achaemenid dynasty that was founded in the seventh century B.C. Early coins and portraits also indicate that pearl pendants were commonly worn in the ears of Persian queens. In India the classic third-century B.C. epic Ramayana describes a precious necklace of twenty-seven pearls, and the pearl drillers whose importance required them to accompany military leaders in a great crusade. Thousands of miles away in China, the *Shu Jing*, one of the earliest books, describes ropes of freshwater baroque pearls from Chinese rivers that were offered as gifts by princes visiting Emperor Yu between 2350 B.C. and 625 B.C. While the Japanese revered pearls less in antiquity, they were aware of them, traded them, and learned about their value. In the early eighteenth century, upon discovering their commercial value, Japanese princes in the pearl-rich Satzuma and Omura provinces quickly banned the sale of pearl oysters in the public fish markets in order to control the supply of these natural gems. Like all rulers, they wanted to keep this source of decoration and currency for themselves.

Rulers possessed the power and the wealth to purchase pearls outright, offer costly and precious goods in exchange for them, or simply seize them by force. However, pearls were not a completely controlled item in the marketplace, and other individuals

In March 1944 photographer Cecil Beaton was under contract with the British Ministry of Information to send back images of Indian life with a positive spin. Apparently, the princess of Berar, wife to the last sultan of the Ottoman Empire, fit the description.

"The aquiline nose, the pointed, pouting lips, the large, lean cheekbones and fierce bird-like eyes were enormously impressive in the manner of primitive sculpture. The wild appearance, though startling, even terrifying, was nevertheless on a grand scale. Magnificent, too, were the enormous drop pearl earrings and her many rows of large pearls," wrote Beaton. The pearls are said to have come from Cartier, although the family has not given the jeweler permission to discuss any of the details. The princess was also known for her fits of temper, often terrorizing shop owners.

"She's highly intelligent and extraordinary looking," said Diana Vreeland. "When you see her wearing these very extraordinary, very exaggerated jewels, you literally think an elephant is entering the room," Vreeland writes about the princess in her book *Allure*, referring to the extraordinary ornamentation of elephants in Eastern countries such as India. "I'm mad about her nose. A nose without strength is a pretty poor performance. It's the one thing you hold against someone today."

could, and did, buy them. When too many subjects wore too many pearls, sumptuary laws were issued in countries such as France, England, Germany, and Italy sought to guarantee that only a select population could flaunt their pearls. In ancient Rome, for example, Julius Caesar initiated laws to limit pearl wearing to members of the ruling court in order to keep the general public from covering themselves with pearls. Augustus Caesar, Caligula (who dressed his horse in a necklace of pearls), and Nero, who sat on a throne covered with pearls and carried a pearl-encrusted scepter, fueled the public's desire for pearls. At the end of the first century Pliny wrote of the Romans: "It is not sufficient for them to wear pearls, but they must trample and walk over them." At few other times in history has the lust for pearls been so pervasive. Everyone, including the

emperor himself, sought pearls in an effort to enlist the gem's mystical allure and to project an image of wealth and status. The lengths to which individuals would go to accumulate pearls were potentially disastrous. For example, the exchange of vast amounts of Roman gold for some of India's pearls is said to have contributed to the fall of this early empire. The quest for pearls in trade-rich Venice between the fourteenth and sixteenth centuries was so great that the Italians finally limited pearl wearing to Venetian women in their first fifteen years of marriage. Only the Doge's wife, daughter, and daughters-in-law were exempt from this law. By 1609 the span was decreased to the first ten years of marriage. When the magistrate also demanded that every other woman surrender her pearls, women kept their real pearls and turned in their copies.

Empress Hirohito and her celebrated pearls.

Apart from the symbolic function that pearls performed for the royals, pearls also represented power as a capital asset. In their natural state, pearls had immediate value and therefore could be used as currency. They could be slipped into a pouch and swept away in the night when a ruler's safety was at stake. Empress Marie-Louise fled in 1815 when the allied armies attacked Paris, and she took with her all of her jewels, including the famous pearl parure—a necklace, earrings, and brooch with a total of 408 enormous pearls—given to her by Napoléon Bonaparte in celebration of the impending birth of their son. When Bonaparte complained, her only concession was to forfeit the necklace to France. On the throne or in exile, pearls were a portable treasury. Later, in 1887, when the French needed to replenish their treasury, they held a landmark sale of the crown jewels. However, the reverse is also true. Many rulers have used their treasuries to purchase pearls. One telling comment was made by a second-century historian about Julius Caesar's purchase of a single pearl for six million sesterces. Suetonius noted that the pearl (which Caesar gave to his mistress, the mother of Brutus) represented "the spoils of nations in an ear, changed to the treasures of a shell."

Although the twentieth-century miracle of pearl cultivation increased the world's supply of pearls—thereby shattering the value of natural pearls—it could not destroy the royal affinity for pearl-laden jewelry. Royal families and titled nobility still wear plenty of pearls, both real and fake. Imitation pearls have existed since the Romans fashioned pearl-like beads of silvered glass. The late Princess Diana wore her Kenneth Jay Lane pearl necklace interchangeably with the more valuable pearls from the vaults of the English crown jewels. After having been robbed, the Duchess of Windsor often wore copies of her dramatically simple natural pearl necklace, and no one knew the difference. The breakdown of exclusivity brought on by the advent of cultured pearls and the increase in the manufacture of imitation pearls has made pearl jewelry accessible on an unprecedented scale. Wearing pearls today attests more to a person's fashion sense than to actual wealth. Whether handed down from a royal treasury or purchased from a street vendor in New York City, pearls retain their regal allegiance to wealth and status. Although pearls were considered the most valuable of all objects during Roman times, it is the Renaissance period that most richly illustrates pearl jewelry and the power of pearls as decorative symbols.

Queen Elizabeth I demonstrated perhaps the most powerful expression of pearls the world has ever known. The vision of the Virgin Queen, as she was called, in her starched lace ruff, long, pointed bodice with a wide farthingale skirt, and ropes of pearls reaching down to her knees, is even more powerful than the pearl-laden images of her father before her. King Henry VIII's padded-shoulder jackets and hats—even his shoes—were encrusted with pearls. Henry's passion for these gems was legendary; many of his pearls were pillaged from the monasteries accumulated during his reign.

Queen Elizabeth I not only inherited her father's appetite for pearls, she absorbed his sense of bravado and showmanship, fusing them into the persona of an earthbound demigod. Elizabeth I understood the art of public spectacle, and no detail escaped her attention: her clothing and makeup, the rose petals strewn on the floor of her yacht, or her frequent village tours that were intended to remind her subjects of their queen's beneficence. Elizabeth gladly spent the hour it could take to attach her ruff and the flounce around the edge of her farthingale.

As the embodiment of virtue, pearls became her trademark and a principal prop in her courtly theatrics. Elizabeth I proclaimed her alliance with purity and chastity by wearing pearls in conspicuous abundance. The queen's obvious attachment to pearls was

This painting of Henry VIII by Hans Holbein shows the Tudor king in full regalia. The pearl ornaments on his hat are known as aglets. These movable ornaments, both jeweled and of solid metals, were worn on hats and other garments, in multiples of two to thirty-six, and Henry's fondness for them helped promote their popularity.

OPPOSITE: Pearls were an indispensable prop in Henry's daughter's highly orchestrated image—where earthly wealth met the ethereal purity of the Virgin Queen. Here Elizabeth I's imposing style and her fixation with pearls are displayed in *The Armada Portrait* (ca. 1588) by George Gower.

an encoded message to suitors and members of Parliament who insisted she marry their monarch: it said that she was "already bound to a husband which is the Kingdom of England." Elizabeth wanted her subjects to believe that she not only ruled by divine will but was herself divine.

Her public persona revolved around an astonishing foundation of pearl adornments. Elizabeth favored ropes upon ropes of pearl necklaces, which were twisted and knotted on top of her pearl-embroidered clothes. In addition to her myriad pearl earrings, mostly pear-shaped drop varieties, Queen Elizabeth I often wore pearl-trimmed hairpieces, which were wired to stand over the head, multistrand bracelets, and jewel-trimmed fans. Even her pet ermine sported a pearl-studded collar! Most of her pearls were the creamy white color we associate with these gems, but some were even rarer black pearls. The queen was fond of mixing white pearls with black. The color combination was symbolic of eternal virginity. When national supplies of white pearls from local rivers and streams dwindled, and when more beautiful specimens acquired via purchase or plunder could not sate her hunger for pearls, the queen bought inexpensive imitations for a penny a piece. Sixteenth-century fakes were made of handblown glass or mother-of-pearl that was filed into beads. With her white facial makeup (a watery paste of egg white, powdered eggshell, alum, borax, poppy seeds, and mill-water intended to bleach her skin) and her pearls, Elizabeth's appearance was not only daunting, it echoed her otherworldly authority.

To maintain her imposing image, the queen had 80 wigs, 125 petticoats, at least 3,000 gowns, and a staff of 6 ladies-in-waiting, plus those of the Royal Office of the Wardrobe of Robes. She employed two full-time tailors and many seamstresses whose sole task was to remove and reembroider the pearls as each item of clothing was cleaned, and to move the pearls from one dress to another because there were never enough pearls to cover all her gowns at once. Elizabeth's wardrobe and jewels were so extensive that they required additional housing at Whitehall, Somerset House, the permanent storeroom at the Tower of London, and a room at the Office of the Wardrobe of Robes. Three hundred carts were required to transport all the leather-covered wooden storage cases from palace to palace.

Possessed by the importance of appearance, Elizabeth hired only attractive people for her household and was known to have rejected one capable applicant because he was missing a tooth. Elizabeth also expected those around her to dress well. But let no woman outshine the queen! When one of her servants, Lady Howard, appeared at court with a sumptuous velvet dress embroidered with pearls, Elizabeth asked to borrow it. Discovering it was too short, the queen proclaimed, "Why then, if it become not me as being too short, I am minded it shall never become thee, as being too fine. So it fitteth neither well."

Elizabeth adored the gifts of clothes and jewels bestowed upon her during tours of her realm and for the annual New Year's Tide, when subjects offered gifts to their monarch. Elizabeth was not above asking nobles to leave lavish gifts to her in their wills. When her friend, the earl of Leicester, died in 1588, he left her a dazzling emerald-and-diamond pendant which hung from a magnificent rope of six hundred pearls. She also received masses of clothes and accessories, which included a pearl-studded swansdown fan. Gifts that Elizabeth did not like or that did not meet her standards were sold, as occurred with pearls she accepted from the countess of Oxford. Gifts of metal were summarily dispensed to the mint.

Although Elizabeth's interest in pearls was legendary, the queen's passion put her in good company. During the Renaissance the expansion of trade between Africa, the Near East, the Far East, and Europe ushered in an era of unprecedented luxury for European elites. The ruling families of Germany, Spain, and Italy, for example, coveted and wore pearls as ornamental badges of superiority.

Catherine de Médicis, a jewelry collector rivaling Queen Elizabeth I, received one of history's most famous gifts of pearls from her uncle, Pope Clement VII, when, at age fourteen (1533), she married the duc d'Orléans, the future King Henry II of France—six ropes of large pearls, strung according to tradition as rosaries or paternosters. Catherine also received numerous pearls from her father-in-law, Francis I, including two loose pearls weighing 92 to 96 grains (or 23 to 24 carats) each, which she wore on her wedding day along with the six pearl necklaces. Francis I was a peacock who had inherited a kingdom of few jewels. He set out to fill France's coffers with gems, and it seems clear that his marriage to Eleanor, the dowager queen of Portugal, was motivated by the desire to gain access to the European nation richest in jewels at that time. By marrying the Portuguese queen, whose trademark ornament was a collar of three rows of pearls set with rubies and diamonds, Francis I accessed a pearl-trading network that extended from India to the Americas. As a result, Francis could choose from some of the world's finest gems to decorate his new daughter-in-law.

Catherine and Henry II interrupted their coronation procession through Paris from time to time so that she might rest from the weight of her jewels. Little did Catherine know that her husband let his mistress wear the crown jewels. Perhaps this indiscretion explains why Catherine willingly gave her pearls to Mary Stuart when Mary married Catherine's son, Francis II. This same collection of six ropes of magnificent round pearls and twenty-five individual large drop pearls, known as the Hanoverian pearls, may have been one of the reasons Queen Elizabeth I had Mary Stuart (the queen of Scotland) beheaded, and subsequently forced Mary's son James VI to sell her the collection for an absurdly low price of 300 pounds sterling. Perhaps James passed them to Elizabeth rather than return them to Catherine, their original owner, because he expected to recoup the pearls, along with Elizabeth's crown, when the Virgin Queen died.

Another pearl with a history of intrigue and drama was discovered during the Elizabethan era, either in the waters off Venezuela or by a slave on Panama's coast (depending upon whose account you believe), and has Elizabeth Taylor as its modern-day guardian. The royal heritage of this pearl, known as La Peregrina, or "The Wanderer" began with King Philip II of Spain, to whom the 203.84-grain pearl (valued then at between 30,000 and 100,000 ducats) was presented by the explorer Don Diego de Temes in 1554. The pearl gift marked the occasion of the matrimony of King Philip II and Mary Tudor I (or Bloody Mary, as she came to be known), who wore the

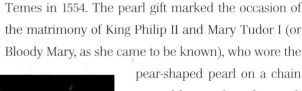

Elizabeth Taylor and Mary Tudor, both wearing the historic La Peregrina pearl.

pear-shaped pearl on a chain around her neck on her wedding day. Queen Margarita of Spain later wore La Peregrina in honor of the peace treaty between Spain and England in 1605. The pearl is said to have appeared on the hat of Philip IV, king of Spain, when he wore it to the wedding of his daughter Maria Theresa and Louis XIV in 1660. La Peregrina left Spain for France, with Joseph Bonaparte's abdication in 1813. Destitute, Prince Louis-Napoléon sold this famous pearl to his friend in London,

the marquis of Abercorn. When Sotheby's put La Peregrina up for auction in 1969, one of the pretenders to the Spanish throne claimed ownership of the pearl and tried in vain to stop the auction. Richard Burton read about the claims in the newspaper, was intrigued, and bought the pearl, via a telephone bid, for $37,000 as a Valentine's Day present for his wife, Elizabeth Taylor. Cartier created a necklace to display the enormous pear-shaped pearl. Rumors suggest that Ms. Taylor may have sold the pearl privately in 1995.

Before the pearl was set as part of the magnificent necklace, La Peregrina was delivered by hand to Mr. and Mrs. Burton by Ward Landrigan, who was then in charge of Sotheby's New York jewelry department. "It was the first big pearl I had ever sold at auction," says Landrigan. "It had a wonderful history. It appears in the Velázquez portraits of the wives of Spain's Philip IV. Then Napoléon owned it. I eventually sold it for the English family. When I delivered the famous pearl to the Burtons, they were staying at the biggest hotel suite you have ever seen in Caesars Palace. The pink shag carpet was at least two inches thick. At three in the morning, after drinking a salty dog—I don't know what a salty dog is, but it had a lot of alcohol in it—we were on our hands and knees crawling around trying to find this pearl. The pearl was lost! I crawled past a pseudo-French settee and there was one of her Lhasa apsos going 'Crunch, crunch.'" Amid growls from the dog, Landrigan retrieved the pearl. "It amused and amazed me that this pearl that had survived wars, famines, and floods had, fifteen minutes into its new ownership, disappeared as a plaything for a dog. The pearl emerged almost unscathed. It had a couple of tiny marks but showed no real damage.

"Actually, La Peregrina seems to have always lived up to its name, the Wanderer, which is how it came to Sotheby's for sale," continues Landrigan. "The pearl fell off of the marquise of Abercorn onto the train of another guest as they were entering the dining room at a ball at Buckingham Palace. The owners eventually found it, but after nearly losing it again at Windsor Castle, and a later near accident, the son had it drilled and set for his wife, but eventually decided to sell it."

The Taylor-Burton story has a fortunate epilogue. Landrigan's wife found, quite by accident, a famous painting of Mary Tudor (by Hans Eworth, dated 1554) wearing La Peregrina. Landrigan alerted Burton, whereupon the Burtons helped purchase the painting and quietly gave it to the National Portrait Gallery in London in 1972. "The gallery has only six or eight Elizabethan portraits," Landrigan adds, "so it is a nice story, don't you think? The Burtons were like that."

During the Renaissance, whether the finest pearls ended up in the jewelry of European courts or Chinese royalty, all the trade routes led back to the very homeland of pearl culture. In *The Book of Pearls* author Joan Younger Dickinson speculates that the quest for pearls began at least as early as 4000 B.C. in the land of Tamil Nadu (what is now southern India, Sri Lanka, and Malaysia), where pearls were found in the Gulf of Mannar, which separates Sri Lanka from India's eastern coast. Korkai, the sophisticated capital of Tamil Nadu, flourished from trade in pearls and conch. The city's substantial revenue fueled its renown as a center of learning and luxury. It was in Tamil that the cult of the shells began, as the pearl represented an effigy of the moon god. Logic suggests that these coastal, seafaring settlers would have used pearls in their ritual worship of the moon god, just as gold's particular qualities and availability made it a natural choice for more inland agricultural communities to use in their worship of the sun god.

India's bounty of pearls—plus its rich deposits of rubies, emeralds, and diamonds—provided the raw material that inspired the development of early Indian jewelry, characterized by a colorful palette and intricate designs, preferences which continue today. Many of the early wall paintings and sculptures, some of which date from the third millennium B.C., indicate that Indian women and men have a long tradition of wearing an abundance of jewels. With its countless versions of hair and turban ornaments, ankle and foot bracelets, even pearls set into an incisor tooth, India has long been resplendent with pearls. Pearls were thought to produce and protect life. A pearl ornament worn on the side of the nose was commonplace, and a typical style of earring was a hoop strung with a trio of pearls. Pendants fashioned from mother-of-pearl were worn on a necklace of leather or hemp. Similar ornaments have been found in ancient Egyptian burial sites and those of North American Indians.

During the early years of the Renaissance, the Italian explorer Marco Polo offered a description of the profusion of pearls that he saw on his travels to southern India. Polo wrote of the king of Malabar, who wore a "rosary" of 104 pearls and rubies around his neck and pearl bracelets and rings on his ankles and toes: "The whole worth more than a city's ransom. And 'tis no wonder he has great store of such gear for they are found in his kingdom. No one is permitted to remove therefrom a pearl weighing more than a *saggio*. The king desires to reserve all such to himself, and so the quantity he has is almost incredible." Throughout history Indians have regarded pearls as prized possessions and, even today, are reputedly less inclined to sell pearls out of their collections.

From the zenith of the Renaissance (coinciding with the reign of England's Henry VIII) until Victorian times, Mughal rulers raised the complexity and richness of ornamentation in India to awe-inspiring heights. Notable for his style and grandeur was Akbar, the grandson of founding Mughal ruler Bābur, who was, in turn, the grandson of the fearsome Mongol conqueror, Genghis Khan. During Akbar's reign, as described by Indian scholar Momin Latif in his book *Bijoux Moghols*, wealth reverted back to emperors when a nobleman died, thus allowing the nobility to live "from day to day in unheeded and unrestrained luxury, where precious gems, pearls and sumptuous jewels occupied a choice place." As an act of piety, Akbar's son, Jahāngīr, wore pearls to his waist and "made a hole in his ears and drew into them a shining pearl." Jahāngīr's son, Shāh Jahān, true to the Indian taste for embellishment, spent seventeen years building the breathtakingly beautiful marble and jewel-inlaid Taj Mahal. The early Mughal rulers' reverence for pearls laid the foundation for the later maharajas, who have come to symbolize the splendor of India. It is impossible not to gasp at

The royal passion for pearls and ceremonial adornment found expression of unequaled splendor among members of the royal families of India, most particularly the men. While such opulence has faded in the recent past, the display was once embraced by young and old. Here, the princely sons of Maharaja Jagatjit Singh of Kakpurthala in turbans and pearls (1890): Mahijit, Karamjit, Amarjit, and Tikka Paramjit. OPPOSITE: **His Highness Jam Sahib of Narajamer, who was known simply as Prince Randi, with a jeweled bird alighting on his headdress and laden with pearls.**

the grandeur of the maharaja of Patiala in a portrait from 1911. The ruler is weighted down with jeweled medals and badges from Anglo-Indian orders, and his *sarpech* (frontal turban ornament) of diamonds and emeralds that was commissioned from Cartier. The maharaja also wears a "sacred thread" of five strands of pearls across the waist, the decorative ropes acting as a regal version of an ancient symbol of caste or social standing, along with a pearl-bedecked turban with a pearl *turra,* or tassel, and a necklace of fourteen strands of natural matched pearls with an emerald-and-pearl pendant centered with the famous Sancy diamond.

While the images of pearl-bedecked Indian maharajas are almost surreal, they illustrate the wealth that has been available to Indian royalty, and give a sense of the historic passion for jewelry in Indian culture. It often seems that Indian men and women wear more jewels than clothing. In fact, they have developed a form of jeweled decoration for almost every part of the body.

"Traditional Indian jewelry is based on the nine planets and nine gemstones, including the pearl," says Viren Bhagat, Bombay's foremost jeweler, who is known for his contemporary jewelry designs incorporating traditional Indian motifs. "I love pearls: the texture, the shades which natural pearls have, the translucence, and the combinations that are possible with diamonds. The pearl signifies the moon, and the moon is the tranquil satellite," Viren continues. "The pearl is used for tranquillity in life and to bring peace of mind. If people suffer from stress, it is recommended that you wear a pearl."

Viren goes on to explain that the maharajas basically signed over their titles and land to India in 1947, when India became independent. Since then, the acquisition of jewelry and the use of jewelry for public display has steadily decreased. "Indian men wear very little jewelry today; mostly it is worn for weddings. Weddings are very elaborate here. Lots of color. Lots of noise."

Wedding celebrations in India can last for three or four days. According to Sudhir Kasliwal, the oldest of the brothers who operate the Gem Palace in Jaipur, established over one hundred years ago as the jeweler to many of the royal families of India, "A wedding dinner for one to two thousand guests is very normal. Here in Jaipur you would see one thousand guests at almost any wedding."

In discussing the royal predilection for pearls, Sudhir observes: "All maharajas had to have jewelry with pearls. When I was born, India had just become independent. I would see maharajas on ceremonial occasions wearing big necklaces with pearls hanging all around. They all had plain pearl necklaces of three to seven rows.

Pearls were used in all the royal jewelry for the beauty of the round and drop shapes." With some regret, he notes, "A lot of the old jewelry has been sold off or auctioned. One family in Jaipur has the most elaborate collection, but you never see it. And there is nothing in museums."

As jeweler to the royal family of Jaipur, Sudhir remains the only person allowed to photograph the *rajmata* (state mother) of Jaipur, Her Highness Rajmata Gayatri Devi. Ayesha, as her friends call her, is the widow of Jai, the maharaja of Jaipur, who was a skilled international polo player and died playing the sport he loved. Currently the eighty-one-year-old, who has hosted every important visitor to Jaipur, including Queen Elizabeth and Jackie Kennedy, lives part of the year in India and part in London. "I am not very jewelry-minded," she emphasizes. "But I have always worn pearls. I had three strings given to me when I got married: two pearl bangles for each wrist, a pearl ring, drop earrings, and three rows of pearls. They were part of my wedding trousseau from Cooch Behar [the state her family ruled]. While I was married, I always wore two strings of pearls. I was known for my chiffon saris—in pink, green, and aquamarine—and pearls around my neck.

"In India," she explains, "people wear a lot of jewelry. When you dress up, jewelry is part of your costume. All stratas of society, from the people in the villages to the people in the palaces, have something on their hands, on their feet, on their necks. It is part of their costume. My mother always wore pearls. I've had other necklaces at times. But I have always worn pearls, natural pearls. My grandmother was the maharani of Baroda, and I can remember the merchants used to come from Basra [a trading center in Iran] and from the Persian Gulf with their pearls. They would come to my family every year in February or March to sell them." In addition to pearls, the *rajmata* also has a *navratna* necklace which she often wears with her pearls. A *navratna* is a necklace or a pendant with all nine gemstones, each representing one of the nine planets. Historically, Indians wore jewelry with all nine gemstones to get the astrological and healing benefits of all the planets.

The term "Basra pearls" stands for natural pearls from the Persian Gulf. According to Sudhir, "a string of 3 mm natural Basra pearls that are perfectly round, with good sheen and good luster, would range in price today from $3,000 to $5,000." A similar Chinese freshwater pearl necklace would cost $50. "The large pearls today are from old family jewelry," he says and, the competition to find that jewelry is steep. No jeweler wants to reveal his sources, and the families do not want anyone to know that they are selling their jewels.

Perhaps only the Russians have embraced pearls with the fervor of the East. Pearls were ubiquitous in Russia; the rivers provided the country with an abundant supply of natural baroque gems. Pearl-encrusted icons date back to the eleventh century, and some of the painted images of the Madonna and Child are aglow from the sea of pearls delineating the shapes. As Baron Haxthausen wrote, "The most respected icons are covered with pearls and gems. . . . It seems that in the Trinity Monastery alone, there are more pearls than in the rest of Europe." Medieval clergy also enjoyed the majesty of pearl embroidery on their vestments, while seed pearl borders as wide as a foot were the hallmark of royal raiment. By the seventeenth century lacy bead-work was part of every Russian woman's wardrobe, typically taking the form of the native headdress, called a *kokoschnik,* which ranged from bouffant to stovepipe to scalloped tiaralike shapes according to region. Catherine the Great instinctively understood the value of incorporating pearls into her public persona, and she won the affection of her people when she appeared in her imperial versions of the *kokoschnik* and peasant dress.

For Catherine, pearls were integral to the fabled excess of czarist Russia, particularly the Romanov style. By the eighteenth century diamonds might have replaced pearls as the fashionable gem for Russians, but pearls were the thread that bound the culture together. Whereas the beautiful empress Elizabeth, who preceded Catherine, amassed more than fifteen thousand dresses of French and Italian styles, Catherine generally preferred a more masculine dress. Perhaps this style of attire best suited her vigorous lifestyle and ambitious plans for her nation. Catherine's fif-teen-hour days began at six A.M., with her usual five cups of strong coffee (which required one pound of coffee beans to brew). Under her reign Catherine expanded Russia's borders by 200,000 square miles; created some one hundred new towns; increased the number of books published each year; and assembled a collection of premier artwork that became the basis for the Hermitage Museum. Catherine saved her personal extravagances for political allies and lovers. Her prime minister and longtime paramour, Grigory Potemkin, used to amuse himself by digging into boxes of pearls and colored gems that Catherine had given him and pouring his largesse from hand to hand with childish glee. Although she owned and wore other sumptu-ous jewelry, Catherine's pearls were of remarkable quality and appear in a number of her portraits. A portrait from her coronation in September 1762, and another by Erichsen, painted after her hair had grayed, show the empress wearing the same

𝒢rand Duchess Alexandra Josifovna (seated left) at
Nicholas II's coronation ball in Moscow with the duchess
of Connaught (daughter-in-law of Queen Victoria).
Behind them, from left to right, are Grand Duchess Vera
Constantinovna; Grand Duchess Anastasia Mihailovna;
Grand Duchess Maria Pavlovna (the elder), who was
Nicholas II's aunt; Grand Duchess Helena Vladimirovna;
Grand Duchess Elisaveta Mavrikievna; and Crown Princess
Victoria of Sweden. Seated on the robes in the foreground
is Duchess Elsa of Württemberg. The gentlemen in the
background are attendants from the *corps des pages*.

This photo was taken May 23, 1896, just hours
after Nicholas II's ascension to the throne at the Kremlin.
It exemplifies the excess and grandeur of czarist Russia.

stately assemblage: a four-strand choker, rising above four descending ropes of hefty pearls, each row centered with a large pearl pendant. The fifth strand is so long that it is knotted near her waist.

Almost one hundred years later Russia's last czar, Nicholas II, gave his child-hood sweetheart, Alexandra, a pink pearl ring and necklace to honor their engage-ment. Alix, also known as Sunny to her grandmother, Queen Victoria, wore the pink gems at her wedding along with a magnificent rope of creamy white pearls the czar commissioned from court jeweler Carl Fabergé for 250,000 gold rubles. For her coro-nation in May 1896 Alexandra wore the pink pearl ring and the necklace alone.

OPPOSITE: *Princess* Alexandra of Denmark married Edward VII (Queen Victoria's son) in 1863, becoming the queen of England in 1901. The high pearl chokers favored by Alexandra were the fashion of the day, but they also served a practical purpose: to conceal a scar on her neck. She was certainly one of the more pearl-intoxicated royals, sometimes wearing up to eleven strands at one time.

Alexandra's lust for jewelry enjoyed a big boost when her husband, then the Prince of Wales, returned from a tour of India with three chests filled with precious gifts including gold, diamonds, and pearls from the maharajas.

Here the Princess of Wales is pictured in cos-tume as Marguerite de Valois, wife of French king Henry IV, for the Devonshire House ball (1897), revealing the excess of fin de siècle Europe, as well as her own extravagant taste.

RIGHT A favorite subject of Baron de Meyer, *Vogue*'s first fashion photographer, was his wife and muse, Olga. In this portrait, taken at Buckingham Palace, Olga is costumed as Queen Alexandra in a gown by Worth and lots of pearls. The baroness was said to be the illegitimate child of Edward VII, although he presented himself as her godfather, and it was Olga who encouraged her husband to perfect his dreamy style of portrait photography.

"Alexandra actually had a spectacular collection of jewelry," explains Romanov jewelry historian Nick Nicholson. "She was just so modest that she is rarely depicted wearing it in any splashy kind of way. She was always giving it away and ordering pieces for the girls, so that they had quite a collection by the time they were sent to Siberia. You can see entry after entry in the imperial registries, which Alexandra always wrote in lavender ink."

The most famous room in the palace was Alexandra's mauve bedroom. Everything was lavender pink, from the Hepplewhite furniture to the endless arrangements of lilacs, roses, orchids, and violets—even the next-door dressing room of closets for her gowns, hats, and trays of jewels. Alexandra preferred pearls to all her other jewels. She wore them alone or with stones, such as sapphires, whichever her gown dictated. But the empress could always be seen wearing the same pearl ropes that cascaded from her neck to her waist.

While their world disintegrated around them in the days before the 1917 Revolution, Nicholas, Alexandra, and their children clung to the vestiges of their imperial luxury. Alexandra wore her pearls amid the chaos, as did her girls.

When Nicholas II, Alexandra, and their children were executed, a portion of the empress's jewels became part of the Bolshevik treasury and some went back to her mother-in-law, the Grand Dowager Empress Marie, who escaped to England, then settled in Denmark, and lived the rest of her life off the periodic sales of her jewels.

In Europe pearls have changed hands as often as treasuries have needed replenishing, and fashions for pearls fluctuated with the fashions for clothing for men and women. Napoléon Bonaparte and his successors, particularly Napoléon III, were formidable players in the court of fashion and jewels. Napoléon I and his daring on the battlefield were echoed by his stylish court. As first consul, a title he earned for life, Napoléon designed his own eye-catching attire that presaged the look of the "dandy"— which included for daytime his gold-embroidered red velvet doublet, short trousers, white silk stockings, and gold-buckled moccasins. His true love, Joséphine, developed a style of her own, discarding the cumbersome layers then in vogue in favor of soft dresses, tied under the bosom with a ribbon that released a flowing skirt. Joséphine's waistless empire silhouette is a look that has passed in and out of favor ever since.

About sixty years later, "the reign of Napoléon III and his Empress Eugénie . . . established Paris once and for all as the international capital of giddily high fashion and delightfully low morals." The

This hand-colored silver print shows Empress Eugénie, wife of Napoléon III, draped in pearls and richly detailed fabrics à l'orientale. The portrait clearly illustrates the empress's love of clothes and jewels.

clothes-mad Eugénie popularized two fashions that parted from the prevailing styles: colored pearls and the *crinoline* (French for "horsehair"). Pearls were a staple in the empress's wardrobe, and she was particularly intrigued by color. Eugénie bought the Tiffany pink pearl found in New Jersey, and she introduced the exotic black pearl to European society.

One of the interesting sidebars to the empress's obsession with fashion concerns her husband's unwavering sexual appetite for Countess de Castiglione. Napoléon III made the sultry brunette his official mistress in 1857, not long after her arrival in Paris at nineteen years of age. He bestowed upon Castiglione a renowned emerald and pearls valued at half a million dollars that were to grace his mistress's neck, along with pearls scattered in her hair, for the rest of her life. Completely self-involved, the Italian countess and would-be actress set a precedent by spending hours cataloging her wardrobe (mostly black and worn with her ever-present pearls), as well as her every mood, in countless photographs.

Even though they were many years apart, Empresses Joséphine and Eugénie had one gift in common: both received important pearls from their Napoléons. The former was more passionate about her husband, the latter about her clothes and jewels, but both empresses understood the beauty of pearls. Joséphine's first gift from Napoléon I was a necklace of three hundred pearls that she wore with

When Marchesa Luisa Casati "ran short of money and a gondolier had to be paid for his services, she would hand him a pearl bracelet," remembered Cecil Beaton.

Her lover, the poet Gabriele D'Annunzio, described her as "pure like fire," and she embodied the spirit of a new Venice in the years preceding the First World War. La Casati, as she was known, knew how to enter a room—which, along with her smouldering eyes and elaborate costumes, earned her the unofficial title of the most extraordinary person in Europe around 1912.

Photographed by Baron Adolph de Meyer, the marchesa drapes herself in pearls alleged to have belonged to another great Italian beauty—the Contessa de Castiglione (opposite), who seduced Napoléon III for reasons of political expediency and received from the emperor this pearl necklace valued at $442,000.

the diamond-studded laurel leaf tiara for her coronation. During a stay at the Plombières spa in the Vosges Mountains of Alsace, Joséphine discovered the irregular beauty of river pearls. She liked them so much that she imported mussels from the Vologne River to the pond at Malmaison in the vain hope of producing home-grown pearls.

Forced to divorce his beloved Joséphine for lack of a male heir, Napoléon I gave his second wife, Marie-Louise, a renowned French pearl of 337 grains (about 84 carats), called La Régente, for her tiara, as well as a parure—a necklace, earrings, and brooch—of 408 pearls, and a few diamonds to celebrate the birth of their son.

Many years later, in 1853, Empress Eugénie wore Marie-Louise's suite for her coronation, even though these particular pearls had a reputation for bringing tears. Eugénie also reset La Régente into a brooch with four pear-shaped drop pearls, each weighing 100 grains (about 25 carats). In the historic public sale of French royal jewels which took place in 1887, Carl Fabergé bought the egg-shaped La Régente pearl for the equivalent of $35,200 and in turn sold it to Russian Princess Zenaïde Youssoupov, who often wore the pearl as a hair ornament or as a pendant for her long pearl sautoir. The pearls belonging to the French treasury and worn by Empress Eugénie sold for 1,261,500 francs (or the equivalent of $252,300).

American millionaire and railroad magnate William K. Vanderbilt bought Eugénie's long necklace of over five hundred pearls for his wife, Alva, who gave them to her daughter, Consuelo, when the Vanderbilts divorced. Mr. Vanderbilt's purchase, along with another pearl necklace, a tasseled rope that had belonged to Catherine de Médicis, was significant because by the second half of the nineteenth century monetary wealth had begun to replace lineage as the measure of respectability. The fall of Napoléon III, followed by the demise of the Russian czars, signaled the end of sovereign rule and traditional aristocracy as it had been known since antiquity. All over

As the aristocracy of Europe was floundering, a new breed of royalty was being minted by America's industrial revolution. Consuelo Vanderbilt, daughter of William K. Vanderbilt, married Richard John Spencer-Churchill, 9th duke of Marlborough, making her the first bridge between new-money society in the United States and titled British nobility. Her mother, Alva, gave her two "fine rows [of pearls] which had belonged to Catherine of Russia and to Empress Eugénie, and also a sautoir which I could clasp round my waist."

For a metaphor for her marriage, look no further than the jewels in this photo of the duchess with her children, John Albert Edward William Spencer-Churchill and Lord Ivor Charles Spencer-Churchill.

$\mathscr{P}$rincess Elizabeth wed Philip Mountbatten on November 20, 1947. This sketch of her dress comes from designer Norman Hartnell. Ten thousand pearls were hand-embroidered on the dress and train in the shapes of the white roses of York, star flowers, corn, and wheat. Even Princess Elizabeth's shoes featured a silver buckle accented with small pearls.

England was economically devastated following World War II, and many feared the public would resent such a display—the dress cost £1,200, the equivalent of £23,000 fifty years later. To the contrary, it became a national dress day, and the streets of London were filled with well-wishers and onlookers.

Princess Elizabeth had been raised on pearls. A necklace of coral beads that she was given by her mother at nine months had pearls added to it by the time she reached age two. For her walk down the aisle, Elizabeth wore the "Crown Pearls," two distinct, graduated strands, each with a pearl clasp—both of which were wedding presents from her father, King George VI. One of the necklaces, with 46 pearls, dates back to Queen Anne (1665–1714); the 50-pearl strand goes back to Queen Caroline (1683–1737). Elizabeth decided on these pearls at the last moment, and her personal secretary, James Colville, had to run through the London crowd to get them from the display of wedding gifts at St. James's Palace, returning just in time for the ceremony.

Europe monarchies were crumbling. A new aristocracy, lead by moneyed American titans such as Mr. Vanderbilt, began to create a broader class of ruling elites. The industrial era allowed individuals, especially Americans, to accumulate vast amounts of wealth—often exceeding royal treasuries—and many of the wealthy Americans lived more like royals than did nobles themselves. Vanderbilt's daughter broke the barriers as the first of the new class of America's privileged millionaires to marry a titled European. As her mother wished, the exquisitely beautiful Consuelo Vanderbilt became the duchess of Marlborough. Consuelo's international image was reflected in pearls: her famous nineteen-strand collar, the lengthy French rope, a pearl crescent brooch, and a pearl tiara for hobnobbing with royalty. When John Singer Sargent painted his famous portrait of Consuelo, the artist removed the duchess's characteristic pearls to reveal her graceful swanlike neck. The portrait was shocking, because not only was it unusual to see Consuelo without her pearls, but as Consuelo recounted in her memoirs, *The Glitter and the Gold*, "one of my sisters-in-law remarked that . . . one should never appear in public without them."

The last of the major dynasties of royal rulers, the current English royal family is perhaps the most visible example of the role priceless jewelry continues to play in the construction of a majestic public image. While Queen Elizabeth II does not rely on the implied voice of purity and divinity that pearls once provided Queen Elizabeth I, she regularly draws on the projected warmth and familiarity of unmistakably grand pearl jewelry, and the potent effect of the imperial collection of more glittering adornment, to lend majestic drama and authority to her civic appearances. And a closer look at the past few generations offers an overview of how the crown jewels and the royal family's jewelry have been incorporated into the wardrobes of one personality after the other.

Down to the quirky diamond miniature crown that she ordered for her personal use, it was Queen Victoria who best understood the symbolic power and the value of imperial jewelry, and she assembled the foundation of the English collection that, to this day, is a historical library of international jewelry design and craftsmanship. Over the sixty years of her reign Victoria spent £157,887 with Garrard, the official crown jeweler (known today as Asprey and Garrard), mostly for royal ornaments. It was Victoria who traced and retrieved much of the missing jewelry from the British treasury, including the famous Hanoverian pearls, which she made a point of wearing for an official portrait so that the world could see that these historic pearls were back under the

Union Jack, where they belonged. Crowned empress of India in May 1876, Victoria received from Indian potentates tributes of unimaginable riches that have provided the bulk of the royal collection and a source of gems for new designs ever since.

Queen Victoria could be as stately as she was romantic. While she could don the most imposing diamond jewels, such as the 161-carat diamond collet necklace of twenty-six individual diamonds as big as lightbulbs, Victoria also could be almost provincial. The sentimental queen always wore her trademark abundance of assorted rings, along with commemorative trinkets such as lockets and the four-strand pearl portrait bracelet from her beloved first cousin and husband, Prince Consort Albert, which she wore until her death. While Albert designed romantic, floral jewelry to go with the lacy romantic clothes he loved on his bride, Victoria's lasting image is her black wardrobe of mourning clothes, embellished with the Order of the Garter and other important jewels. But the barely five-foot queen could often be seen simply accenting the black with some of her favorite ropes of pearls.

As queen consort, Victoria's daughter-in-law, Alexandra, borrowed from both Elizabeth I and India in fashioning her own aesthetic of self-adornment. For her husband's coronation, Alexandra bedecked herself in jewels: her signature four-row pearl dog collar; seven strands of large pearls graduating in length from 24 to 30 inches; a diamond choker and a pearl-and-diamond brooch from her husband, Edward VII, known as "Bertie," sporting three pear-shaped pearls that had once belonged to Napoléon. In fact, for the coronation, Edward VII declared that only the royal family could wear crowns of pearls. Bertie's own crown was topped with pear-shaped pearl drops that were actually Queen Elizabeth I's pearl earrings, their fittings and all. Although Alexandra wore her collar of pearls to cover the scar on her neck, a vestige of a childhood illness, collars of this type quickly became the fashion, one that would be continued by her successor, Queen Mary, whose elegance inspired Princess Diana.

Along with the brooch, King Edward VII gave his bride a necklace of diamond-encircled pearls connected by swags of diamonds and three drop pearls that continues to be a favorite of the Queen Mother. From her father, King Christian IX of Denmark, Alexandra also received the famous Dagmar necklace as part of her dowry. This necklace is a scrollwork piece consisting of 2,000 diamonds and 118 sizable pearls, including a diamonds-and-pearls pendant in the shape of an eleventh-century Dagmar cross. Worn without its cross, this crown jewel is a favorite of England's current Queen Elizabeth.

Even in mourning, Queen Victoria often wore her tasseled pearl sautoir and favorite pearl bracelets.

About the time that Alexandra married Bertie, her sister Marie married the next-to-last czar of Russia, Alexander III. When Marie escaped the Russian Revolution in 1917 and fled to Copenhagen to the holiday retreat that she and her sister shared, it was Bertie and Alexandra's son King George V who took care of his aunt and her jewels, which were valued at nearly a million dollars in 1923 (about eight million dollars today).

Queen Mary helped herself to a hefty share of the prize Russian jewels, insisting that the Depression had reduced their value and paying only a fraction of their value to Marie's heirs. Queen Mary, formerly Princess May of Teck, who was rechristened Mary when she was forty-three years old, entered the royal family with proper royal connections but no financial backing. Armed with her father's passion for collecting and arranging and a few jewels of her own, the Queen Consort was soon to buy, inherit, copy, even cajole from her late brother's mistress, a collection of jewels that is still in view. For her wedding Mary took her cues from her mother-in-law and wore a pearl-and-diamond tiara along with her signature pearl-and-diamond choker, which was eleven-strands deep, and a long pearl sautoir. Later, Mary acquired her beloved four-strand pearl collar from Empress Maria Feodorovna's fabled jewelry collection and some of the jewels of Grand Duchess Maria Pavlovna, which had also been smuggled out of St. Petersburg and included the fabled circle tiara. As an alternative to the original hanging pearls in the overlapping diamond circles, Mary provided interchangeable emeralds.

The British attachment to pearls continues today. Even as Lady Elizabeth Bowes-Lyon, the Queen Mother was known for her pearls. Her childhood wardrobe of jewels consisted of a seed pearl necklace which she wore constantly and a string of small coral beads. Today the Queen Mother still wears pearls, lots of them. And, as with many of her favorite pieces, she wears the same pearls over and over again. Countless photographs show the rather dainty woman in the double strand of her younger years with its pearl drop; the pearl mesh sautoir with jeweled diamond stays on either side, given to her as a wedding present by the citizens of London; her ubiquitous double- and triple-strand combinations by day; the Diamond Jubilee pin with center pearl and pearl drop that was presented originally to Queen Victoria in 1897 by her household; and her favorite, Princess Alexandra's necklace of diamond-encircled pearls connected by swags of diamonds and a trio of pearl drops.

Princess Anne borrows the pearl-and-diamond choker that once belonged to Empress Maria Feodorovna and was originally commissioned by Queen Mary. The present queen wears the four-row pearl bracelet with a sapphire-and-diamond clasp that Queen Victoria had had made from a necklace, a piece that was also a favorite of Victoria's daughter-in-law Queen Alexandra. And the pearls keep going around and around, providing pageantry, majesty, and continuity from reign to reign, fashion to fashion, cultural ideology to ideology.

The Queen Mum wears a chestful of her many signature pearl necklaces and the diamond fringe tiara that Queen Victoria left to the Crown.

TRADITI

You can turn an absolute whore into a lady by just putting pearls around her neck," declares fashion designer Donald Brooks. While the metamorphosis from streetwalker to chair of a benefit ball may assign too much power to the pearl, Brooks's comment contains a grain of truth about the transformative qualities of attire that the designer has learned very well. Throughout his career, Brooks has used clothing to create illusions, and reveal truths, about the identities of those he dresses. For society women like Nancy Reagan and Lady Keith, and celebrities like Joanne Woodward, Diahann Carroll, Liza Minnelli, Judy Garland, Barbra Streisand, Julie Andrews, and Carol Burnett (for whom he created an all-pearl minidress for her role as

ONALISTS

an ingenue-goes-to-Hollywood in the musical *Fade Out, Fade In*), Brooks's art has helped them to convey power and prestige, glamour, or even comedic effect. When selecting accessories for his clients, Brooks keeps an age-old axiom in mind: "The unwritten rules of propriety, passed down from mother to daughter for generations, have stated that 'a lady isn't a lady without her pearls.' The implication is that pearls are the badge of the proper woman, and 'proper' translates as traditional."

"But times change," he concedes. "One day the walnut-sized South Sea pearls are in fashion and the next day it's the little seed pearls in delicious colors. No matter what size, shape, or color, though, pearls will weather the tides of fashion to remain the gift of choice among traditionalists."

At the same time that Brooks was designing for entertainers and social luminaries, retailers were finding that the American Everywoman too regarded pearls as signifiers of traditional classic taste. "Pearls were the first thing we reached for when we accessorized, whether it was a customer, a display, or models for a fashion show," says Gerald Blum, former executive vice president of marketing for New York's Lord and Taylor department store. "Lord and Taylor was a traditional store, and our customer base was women who wore pearls. These women were intelligent, attractive, educated, and had a sense of beauty about them, as pearls do. Pearls were an integral part of their backgrounds. In fact, pearls and women often seemed interchangeable."

PAGE 78: *Nancy* Reagan, who has always worn pearls, says that Ronald Reagan gave her this pearl necklace. Here she wears it to a Hollywood nightclub in 1957. The pearl earrings were a staple for Mrs. Reagan in the early years of their marriage.
RIGHT: Sid Luft bought Judy Garland this pearl bracelet in the early sixties while they were still married. "Judy wasn't fascinated by jewelry. She had very simple taste, but she loved pearls," says Luft. "She wore them all the time. It's a delicate material that has an almost ethereal quality when you see the shine. And the rainbow—maybe that's what she liked about them. The ring was a gift from a wealthy fan from Long Island who knew that Judy loved pearls and sent it to her."

The intelligence and beauty of the women Blum describes are qualities that define all the traditionalists that this chapter illustrates. The *way* of being traditional, however, can take several forms. There is the plainspoken, quietly confident variety embodied by such women as Barbara Bush, Coretta Scott King, and Helen Keller. Gertrude Vanderbilt Whitney, the duchess of Windsor, C.Z. Guest, and Lady Diana Manners Cooper represent the aristocratic, cosmopolitan traditionalists. A new traditionalist has developed over the years to embrace the often-pioneering women who are united by a stable set of core values, but who are not afraid to raise some eyebrows as they broaden the traditional roles of women. Pearls are the uniform of the traditionalist, whether she was born into the role and has had pearls handed down to her, or whether she adopted traditional values and learned about the importance of wearing pearls.

*B*lind, deaf, and mute from her infancy, Helen Keller became an icon of heroism and triumph of the human spirit over adversity. Her early education with her teacher, Anne Sullivan, was dramatized in the 1962 film *The Miracle Worker*.

Ms. Keller was photographed in Paris in 1950 while reading the lips of her traveling companion, Polly Thomson. She was meticulous about her appearance—she wouldn't go out without a hat; and the inventory sheet for the jewelry she brought on this European voyage was several pages long. Among the items were three different triple-strand cultured pearl necklaces, one of which contained pearls that were a healthy 9.5 mm in size.

RIGHT: **Coretta Scott King, adorned with a pin and elegant drop-pearl earrings.**

"Pearls make you feel secure when you are wearing them," says Lyn Williams, a highly respected civic leader based in New York City and Sag Harbor. "And when you see someone else wearing pearls, you assume they share a certain set of traditional values; that they are solid and reliable. Initially, I would feel a little more relaxed and open."

Perhaps better than any other accessory, pearls signal assurance, substance, and groundedness, and as such are an invaluable tool to anchor a woman's wardrobe for traditional professions. Many nonwork occasions too warrant the gem that seems universally to communicate a decorous attitude. Lyn Williams speaks to this issue: "Pearls have a certain aura about them, something that is very basic and right. They are classic and correct. You know that you are okay if you have on your pearls. A lot of social rules have been changed, twisted, or dropped, but there are certain times when being correct is still important. When you walk down the aisle to be married, when you go to the interview with the co-op board, or when you go to a funeral, you can't go wrong with pearls."

Having received pearls from her mother, father, and husband, Lyn is expressing the common bond between pearls and the traditionalist, which is telegraphed through outward appearance. Traditional

Bert Williams with an elegant pearl tiepin, the traditional way for men to adorn themselves with pearls. OPPOSITE: **Mrs. William Hayden English Walling, at home in Paris, in a Schiaparelli dress and family pearls.**

grooming is, in a way, straightforward and reassuring. Though there is as much room for experimentation and creativity on one end of the traditional wardrobe spectrum as there is for understated, classical styles on the other, it is a given that all that comprises these personal styles will be of the highest caliber—fine fabrics and workmanship, first-rate designers and dressmakers, and quality accessories, whether real or faux. The natural, subtle beauty of pearls completes the package.

The traditionalist is devoted to family and community and is dedicated to stability and order. The power of traditionalists in our society lies in their ability to assure us of a steady and orderly life. "I think we are going back to tradition," says trendspotter and consumer expert Faith Popcorn. "We always turn to established values in times of flux. Right now we are having the millennium shakes and are turning to traditions to assuage this anxiety. To preserve the order. It shouldn't mean going backwards, which we tend to do. It means preserving the best of the past and taking it forward in a seamless fashion. That's why Ralph Lauren has made millions. It's why Oreo cookies have survived. Or Lincoln Logs and Dr. Seuss. And passing down pearls from mother to daughter, or in my case, grandmother to granddaughter."

Faith's grandmother Rose wore a flapper-length rope of pearls, doubled into a shorter necklace, every day. She passed them on to Faith, who then wore them every day for years; Faith plans to leave them to her recently adopted daughter, "G.G."

Passing on personal belongings "is a variation of one of the ten truths of marketing to women," explains Faith. "Women pass brands down through the generations. This generation of female consumers will lead you to the next, because women look for relationships and ties that go beyond the product. Pearls offer that implied bond."

If, as Faith Popcorn suggests, we are looking to traditions to ease our anxieties in this era of rapid change, who better to look to for reassurance than one of our most maternal First Ladies? It is difficult to imagine Barbara Bush without her pearls. Pearls have helped Mrs. Bush convey her human, practical, and unpretentious brand of traditionalism. As First Lady, she wore pearls all the time. In fact, she invariably wore the same style necklace. Owing to her public role, Barbara Bush, in her three-strand necklace of eighty-eight hand-knotted glass pearls by Kenneth Jay Lane, was a constant presence in the media throughout her years as First Lady, and still is. Although she has left the White House, she hasn't given up her pearls. Pearls became her hallmark, though Mrs. Bush admits, "I didn't choose pearls as my signature. It just happened."

While she was known to have borrowed important jewelry for the stage, and liked jewelry, the soprano Maria Callas was photographed frequently in pearls. Here she wears a multi-strand necklace in a portrait by Cecil Beaton.

In the family tradition, Lily Auchincloss enjoys playtime with her granddaughter, Lily. Lily senior is wearing a South Sea pearl necklace and signature X-shaped pearl earrings from New York society jeweler Christopher Walling.

OPPOSITE: "The women on my side of the family all had pearls that were handed up and down and sideways throughout the family," says New York decorator Lithgow Osborne. "They were cut up and, years later, put back together. The number never changed, just the configuration. It was a very big day when my sister got her string of pearls from my mother." Lithgow takes a tour of the portrait of his cousin, Marietta Tree, and her family by The Right Honorable the earl of Lichfield. Clockwise from Penelope Tree at the top: "Whatever Penelope is wearing, I know they're not real. At that time she had never owned a piece of real jewelry. She loves it, but things like pearls and tradition are not her style." Author Frances FitzGerald without pearls. "Marietta has on the triple-strand choker given to her by her first husband, Desmond FitzGerald. And my aunt (Mrs. Malcolm Endicott Peabody)—every time I saw her she was wearing those damn pearls. They were part of her; an amulet of sorts to ward off the evil spirits."

Pearls are an accessory that have surrounded Mrs. Bush since youth. "I have always worn pearl necklaces," she attests, "having received my first strand when I was sixteen." Those pearls were real. When her husband, George, was U.S. ambassador to the United Nations, Mrs. Bush's friend Princess Catherine Aga Khan introduced her to jewelry by Mr. Lane. Kenny, as he is known to his friends and business acquaintances, raised the standards for style and quality in costume jewelry. Kenny's classical forms, combined with mass-market pricing and his charismatic personality—social bravado infused with levity—proved to be a successful business formula that began in the 1960s. One of his specialties is faux pearls. Kenny's pearls had already been discovered by Jackie Kennedy and Nancy Reagan. However, as First Lady, Barbara Bush made Kenny's classical pearls part of her public image. At her husband's request after his election as vice president, Mrs. Bush set about developing an appropriate wardrobe for official duties. Mrs. Bush admits in her biography that such an authoritative wardrobe had not been a priority in her life. New York fashion designer Arnold Scaasi added refinement to her clothing, and Kenny's pearls brought her personal style into focus. "Conservative at first," Kenny writes in his autobiography, "she bought five strands of small pearls." By the time she stepped into her shoes as First Lady, she graduated to the larger 12mm pearls that balanced her full white hairstyle, highlighted her smile, and underscored her maternalistic style.

Mrs. Bush wears four versions of her necklace, each with a different clasp (a gold-loop closure, one with rhinestones, another with crystals, and a fourth with rubies and crystals). Though the actual necklace Mrs. Bush wore to her husband's

Girls in their pearls: (from the left) First Ladies Nancy Reagan, Lady Bird Johnson, Hillary Clinton, Rosalynn Carter, Betty Ford, and Barbara Bush gathered for "A Tribute to America's First Ladies" at the U.S. Botanic Garden in 1994.

OPPOSITE: Just hours before a 1989 state dinner at the White House, First Lady Barbara Bush—dripping in Kenneth Jay Lane costume pearls—poses for Harry Benson. "She always wore pearls," says Benson. "They gave her a kind of glamorous look. She also helped the picture by bringing Millie (her English Springer spaniel)."

presidential inauguration resides in the Smithsonian Institution in Washington, D.C., duplicates of the quartet of pearl chokers that Mrs. Bush continues to wear, along with matching pearl earrings, are available for sale at the Bush Library in Texas.

In addition to her white pearl jewelry, Kenny made a necklace of black pearls for Mrs. Bush to wear to the funeral of Japanese Emperor Hirohito in 1989. In the rush to complete the necklace in time for the funeral, everyone forgot about matching earrings. Kenny quickly fabricated the black pearl earrings, but as he relates, "Even Federal Express couldn't get them to the White House in time for a five-thirty A.M. departure. The last shuttle flight from New York to Washington saved the day."

In contrast to the more populist appeal of Mrs. Bush and her pearls is the aristocratic, genteel traditionalism of C.Z. Guest and Babe Paley, for example. These women might have individual eccentricities, but their identities revolve around preserving a traditionally elegant way of life. Their pearls mirror a style predicated on the finest of everything: fine tailoring, fine detailing, and fine jewelry. No need to shout out their wealth or power; no need for overstated clothes or pearls.

"There are things I like much better than jewelry," confesses C.Z. Guest, the garden columnist, entrepreneur, and quintessential American pearl wearer: "Horses, my late husband, Winston, my children, my dogs. For birthdays or Christmas my husband always gave me fantastic horses. I'd rather have any of those things than a diamond necklace. But I've always had pearls," she confides. "As a young girl, I had a little pearl necklace, and my parents gave me two or three pearls for every birthday; I started my daughter, Cornelia, like that too. Now I have my mother's natural pearl necklace," she continues. "It started off as two strands, then I added the third. My mother contributed some, my husband gave me some, and when Mother died, she had some big pearls that I put right in the middle. Pearls dress up even a simple little black dress or an evening gown. A gold necklace is nothing, but put a strand of pearls on, and it changes the whole look. Very ladylike, which is something we have forgotten today. You can't go wrong with pearls. More and more people are wearing them. With all the cultured pearls today, anybody

C.Z. Guest was one of the most famous debutantes of 1937–1938. Her pale blue eyes, pale blond hair, and disciplined figure made her one of the great beauties of the productive period after the war. Her marriage to Winston Frederick Churchill Guest underscored her place in the international horsey set. For years she wore only clothes by Mainbocher, appreciating the beautiful fabrics and workmanship. Diana Vreeland said of the dress she wears in this portrait, by Louise Dahl Wolfe, that it was one of the most beautiful dresses she had ever seen. Mrs. Guest added her own pearl necklace and bracelet.

can have some," says the elegant matron, who herself sports a choker of rather weighty ones of the cultured variety.

In addition to embellishing one's wardrobe—and Guest's voice sparkles when she points out this other potent charm of pearls—the gems flatter the woman herself. "Pearls are so seductive and beautiful. They are the most feminine of all the jewels; men certainly can't wear them," says the woman who decided many years ago that pearls were her natural jewel. "They are alive on the skin. Really. Especially for women like me, with blond hair, blond skin, and blue eyes. After all, you want to be feminine and desirable. That's the point of a beautiful woman. All the great love stories, poems, and beautiful music were written for beautiful women. That's what it's all about."

Elvin McDonald, gardener laureate, senior staff editor, and garden editor of *Traditional Home* magazine, says of Guest, his longtime friend, "Of all the people I have ever known, she is the definition of beauty in the same way as a pearl is." In 1975 he was sent to interview Mrs. Guest on the occasion of the publication of her debut book, *First Garden.* McDonald admits he had the impression that Mrs. Guest was going to be an "emerald-breasted dowager," until he met her. "People have always looked upon her as rich and spoiled. People mistakenly think that old, deep wealth means not doing anything for one's self, when in fact she was the one who did everything. She is extremely disciplined. She exercises every day. And she keeps everyone in the household going. She believes in self-control. She might describe herself as an old lady, but nothing can get around the fact that she is an exceptional beauty. There is hardly anyone who has retained that beauty throughout her life."

Lady Sarah Churchill grew up in the culture of pearls, and she expresses an emotional connection to these sea-born gems: "When I go out, I feel undressed if I don't have my pearls on. If I start to leave for dinner and they are not on, I have to

*T*own & Country magazine, on the cover if its June 1956 issue, paid tribute to the broader incorporation of French food and elegance into American culture during this defining era of etiquette. In a single day the following patrons dined at Henri Soulé's brilliant Le Pavillon restaurant in New York: (top) the duchess of Windsor and the Marquesa Alfonso de Portago; (middle) the Viscountess Paul de Rosière and Alfred Hitchcock; (bottom) Mrs. John C. Wilson and Noël Coward.

turn around, go back, and get them. My pearls are my security blanket. I live in the country and don't wear them every day." With refreshing candor and common sense, Lady Sarah describes her protocol for jewelry wearing: "I just wear pearls: a necklace—three strings of real pearls—and fake pearl earrings."

"My grandmother gave me pearls every year for my birthday and Christmas," she reflects. "As I got older the pearls got bigger, and I ended up with two strings. I bought the short row to make it three," she says, adding that "there is no point in having real pearl earrings because you take one off to make a telephone call and there it goes. If you buy good fake pearls, half the world doesn't even know they aren't real. Then when they start to peel, you throw them away and get another pair. I am also very keen on my big pearl-and-gold ring. It is easy to wear and not the sort of thing that means you are going to get your hand cut off for wearing it. I don't go into New York in my diamond ring—which is made from my grandmother's large stone, two other diamonds from my mother, and some tiny diamonds from my christening bracelet—I think it is too dangerous to do so.

"Everybody thinks my pearls were my grandmother's, but I gave hers to my daughter, who is also named Consuelo. Knowing her, they are in a vault somewhere!" says Churchill, bemusedly. Lady Sarah Churchill's mother's pearl necklace, which she describes as made of "big, big heirloom pearls, just about sweater neckline in length," now belong to her sister-in-law, Rosita, the current duchess of Marlborough, because according to British inheritance traditions, family valuables are passed down through the male heirs. "I think Rosita only wears those pearls on very special occasions. I think they live in a box. That is not good for pearls; they need to be worn," says Lady Churchill, who wears her own pearls enough to keep a proper patina, and maintains that she has her pearls restrung, "more or less religiously," every two years.

Charlotte Ford for years has settled matters of etiquette in her magazine columns and books. In true traditionalist form, Ford's first pearls were natural Add-A-Pearls which she received, a few at a time, until she had one long rope that could be worn as one or two strands. However, as an adult, she turned to imitations. "I don't like to travel with real jewelry," says Ford, who in many ways epitomizes the modern traditionalist. "The faux pearls are a little bit bigger. I like them and own quite a few pairs. I look for the pearls that are not too white or too yellow in color, but somewhere in between, so they don't look too plastic on my skin. I have earrings I like to wear too, which have to match the necklace, or at least be close in color." Ms. Ford wears her necklace, earrings, and a single-strand bracelet all together when wearing a suit or a dress. Recently Ms. Ford has come to enjoy natural pearls again, however, and reveals that she often considers exchanging the "very, very dressy" diamond bracelet her mother left her, for a beautiful pearl necklace. Whether they are real, or just really good fakes, Ford says, "pearls work for me because they go with everything. They really do. Even a really small strand can go on top of a T-shirt. I love pearls and have always felt that way. I think pearls are very glamorous," she concludes.

Growing up among Venezuela's elite, New York fashion designer Carolina Herrera gained a keen understanding of her social clientele. A traditionalist herself, Herrera lives much as her clients do, which helps make her a favorite with modern traditionalists and their daughters. When asked to consider her taste in accessories, Herrera says she likes her pearls to have a little drama. "I do wear pearls in my ears, every day. It took a long time to find the right size pearl. They are not huge spheres, but they are big. I like big pearls. In the daytime I keep it simple. I might wear one strand of pearls or two little ones, but usually just the earrings. I wouldn't wear the necklace and earrings together. In the evening I wear a lot of jewelry, something chic and noticeable. I would wear the pearl necklace with diamond or emerald earrings." Herrera identifies one quality unique to pearl jewelry: their tasteful, unassuming luxury. "There is never an excess in pearls," she concludes. "You can wear a lot of them and they look absolutely fantastic. I love the baroque pearls. The shapes are so beautiful; quite exotic. I like their texture and the way they refract the light. It is very fashionable now to have a baroque necklace.

"My first present was a little pearl necklace, when I was maybe fifteen years old; a very small necklace of tiny pearls. Creamy, round ones from the island of Margarita, which is just off the coast of Venezuela," continues Mrs. Herrera. "Likewise, I gave my daughters little pearl earrings and a little necklace. All of my pearls have come from my family or were gifts from my husband. One is always in the bank, while I wear the other one. I inherited marvelous pearls—cream-colored ones—from my grandmother, and I wore them all the time. And my husband gave me a very beautiful pearl necklace. Very white. I enjoy wearing them for him. I think men like jewelry more than women. They like it because they cannot wear it, and you always admire something that you cannot have. It is very nice when you are older to wear pearls. Look at Mrs. Bush; she looks wonderful."

Carolina Herrera, who lives in pearls by day, is celebrated in all of her timeless elegance in this image by Robert Mapplethorpe.

Socialite Nan Kempner holding court at the Metropolitan Opera's 100th Anniversary Gala in 1984. "My pearls are from JAR in Paris," says Mrs. Kempner, "all twisted with a pin and a ruby in the middle. They are two long strands, which I'll wind long or short. I can wear them around my neck or around my wrist. I can use them as a belt. They're quite versatile."

Seated to Nan's left are Fran Stark and couturière Jacqueline de Ribes. While the elegant French countess occasionally wears colored gems, she prefers pearls with diamonds. "They are my favorite mixture," she confirms. "The bow on my shoulder is part of a tiara that belonged to my husband's family. It's the centerpiece fleur de lis of diamonds and pearls. Countess de Ribes designed her own drop earrings of diamond-encircled pearls for this celebration.

New York socialite Nan Kempner, like Mrs. Herrera, is another woman who likes to make a little statement with her jewelry. "I got a lovely, very ladylike little strand of pearls for my sixteenth birthday," she says, "and from then on in I went into biggies. I love scale. I can't stand little bitsy jewelry. I would rather not have any at all.

"Years ago," she recounts, "my husband, Tommy, asked me what I wanted for my birthday. As a joke, I said that I wanted a strand of pearls that reached from the bed to the door. And I got it! Two long strands. You could put them together and take them apart. They were marvelous. I wore them coiled like a rope or down to my knees. Later on, when my mother died, I threw her diamond necklace into it. David Webb made rondelles, so every three or four pearls, there were good, chunky diamonds. Of course they vanished, along with my mother's pearls and everything else," she says wistfully. Mrs. Kempner did not put her jewelry in the safe the last day of the opening of the Las

Hadas resort in Mexico, and while she was playing tennis, the jewels were stolen. This was the first of three robberies for her. The last was an armed robbery in her own apartment, which left her handcuffed to the towel bar and apologizing to the criminals for the paucity of quality pieces—most had already been stolen. The police caught one set of villains when they tried to sell the jewelry back to her husband. "The pearls are the thing I really miss. They were easy to wear. A simple white cotton shirt looked very grand when I put on my pearls.

"Since then I have managed to collect very nice pearls," she says, brightening, "and I am lucky to have what I have. Tommy says he hates giving me jewelry now. He feels like he is renting it"—she shrugs—"because it always ends up in someone else's hands." Mrs. Kempner ticks off her pearl larder: a large white pearl necklace that she bought at Fred Leighton, a separate pearl drop from Verdura jewelers, and black pearls that Tommy found at the November 13, 1995, "Jewels from the Personal Collection of Princess Salimah Aga Khan" sale at Christie's in Geneva. Her favorite way to wear them: in the buff.

The designer of the renowned jersey wrap dress, Diane von Furstenberg, is a good example of the new breed of independent traditionalist. She educated herself on sound business principles that, combined with creative savvy and her instincts for trends, generated a small fortune. "Pearls are very womanly. They are very reassuring, and a pearl necklace with earrings is an ideal combination of jewelry," says Diane. "I bought my first pearls some twenty years ago in Hong Kong. I saw them in the beginning of the trip—big South Sea baroque pearls—and by the end of my travels, regretted that I hadn't bought them." So she inquired and found that the pearls were still for sale, ordered them, and then wore them constantly. After talking about pearls for this book, she has decided to start wearing them again.

Another modern traditionalist who bought her own pearls is Shahara Ahmad-Llewellyn, the New York

In the foreground, designer Diane von Furstenberg relaxes at home as Andy Warhol's triptych image of her looms overhead. "Pearls are the ideal piece of jewelry. They are very womanly," says the designer whose wrap dresses have become reliable basics, and backdrops for pearls, for two generations of women.

"Pearls make me feel good," Ms. von Furstenberg continues, "even if I hide them in a sweater. They are reassuring. They have a life of their own. They are alive. I also believe they bring good luck."

philanthropist and businesswoman who, together with her husband, Bruce, owns the Philadelphia Coca-Cola Bottling Company. "One day, I looked around and everyone was wearing these giant pearl necklaces," exclaims Shahara. "The beautiful, ladylike pearl necklaces like the one that Bruce gave me when we were married were suddenly obsolete. I asked Bruce for new pearls, and he said he was out of the pearl business. He was buying art. So I bought my own pearls; I have my own money. On a trip to Tokyo in 1982, when you could still afford 14 mm pearls, I bought a choker, another strand to fit around it, and two long ropes."

The modern-day traditionalists discussed thus far have built upon a rich legacy of pearl wearers who preceded them. It is interesting to look back at some of the traditionalists who have left their marks on the history of style, particularly those who lived in the period between the end of the nineteenth century and the start of World War II. During this time women—especially wealthy and often titled socialites—worked at developing their own style of dress, entertaining, and living. Whether English, French, or American, they crossed paths regularly and ultimately, often through their very eccentricities, helped effect the transition from the rigidly aristocratic, traditional Edwardian society to the more open café society.

One such group in Paris, known as Les Dames de Vogue, captured the public's imagination under the leadership of American transplant Daisy Singer Decazes de Broglie Fellowes, a woman renowned for her jewelry, particularly her awe-inspiring pieces from Cartier, Schlumberger, and Van Cleef and Arpels, among others. Mrs. Fellowes had a penchant for buying jewels in pairs, such as matching bracelets, because she loved the symmetry a twosome provided.

Meanwhile, Lady Diana Manners Cooper, the well-known beauty, was London's beacon of style before she moved to Paris when her husband was appointed Britain's ambassador to France. In contrast to the free-spirited fashions of Les Dames, the refined style of the duchess of Windsor also attracted its own set of international disciples. In New York and Paris, where she spent part of each year during the early years of the twentieth century, socialite Rita de Acosta-Lydig, created a sensation when she appeared at the opera in the first backless dress. While the mesmerizingly beautiful Mrs. Lydig devoted her life to the pursuit of aesthetics, Gertrude Vanderbilt Whitney combined her passion for the arts with personal finances and social clout to found the Whitney Museum of American Art. The chokers, ropes, and multiple strands of

Industrialist George Jay Gould married actress Edith Kingdon in 1886, two years after he saw her in a play. This rope of matched Oriental pearls was a gift to her from her husband. The style of the day dictated a long rope, and Mrs. Gould's fashionable noose was dubbed "the Million-Dollar Pearls"—after the price quoted by Tiffany in the late 1800s.

Since it was not appropriate for a woman of her status to appear in the theater, Mrs. Gould brought the theater to herself. For a Christmas party in December 1899, Edith commisioned three plays, and starred in one called *The Twilight of the God.* The description of her taken from Edwin P. Hoyt's *The Goulds: A Social History,* applies here: "Mrs. Gould . . . wore a low-cut ball gown of lace-trimmed white satin that revealed new aspects of sizable breasts and her wasp-waist. Around her neck was the $500,000 string of pearls."

$\mathcal{D}$olly Hoffman, in her Art Deco necklace from Cartier. Known for her invincible style, she acquired the necklace before she married the architect Francis Burrall Hoffman (who designed James Dearing's Villa Vizcaya in Miami). Couturier Hubert de Givenchy remembers her as the chicest woman he has ever known. OPPOSITE: One half of the biggest dance sensation in the world from 1911 to 1918, Irene Castle was a style leader of the nascent Jazz Age and can be credited for introducing bobbed hair. As *The Christian Science Monitor* observed at the time, Irene and her husband, Vernon Castle from England, "showed and taught people of two continents how modern dances ought to be danced. They eliminated vulgarity and replaced it with refinement." They opened a dance school, called Castle House, where they introduced the tango, the hesitation waltz, and the fox-trot to New York's blue bloods. Naturally, pearls were in the picture, like the fashionably long rope worn by Irene in this portrait by Cecil Beaton. But she also used pearls in inventive ways, starting a style that remains emblematic of the 1920s; called "the headache band," it was a piece of velvet ribbon beaded with small pearls and worn around the forehead.

pearls of this global sorority of traditionalists spoke of a privileged social station and a commitment to preserving a lifestyle of gentility, even as the lines between the classes began to blur.

Diana Manners Cooper flourished in the dichotomy of her elite social status and the carefree bohemian culture to which she was drawn. A devoted and loyal friend to many, Diana loved people and loved to see them have a good time. During her famous soirées, she made use of her stage-acting experience, delighting guests with her outlandish costumes and impersonations. She also cultivated artists as friends, and so party goers might find Artur Rubinstein at the piano or Fyodor Chaliapin singing in her parlor. Although she was an outspoken adventuress and an eccentric, she nonetheless was adored by traditional society, who followed her every move and eagerly awaited her social invitations.

Born to a duke and raised to be a duchess, Diana grew up in a manor house with tutors and all the requisite trappings of the aristocracy. Her artistically inclined mother instilled in Diana an inquisitiveness and independence that coalesced into a magnetic allure and zest for adventure that gathered momentum during the course of her life. From her travels, to her black-painted bedroom strewn with swags of flowers, Diana's originality was the inspiration for literary characters, such as her friend Evelyn Waugh's Mrs. Stitch, D. H. Lawrence's Lady Artemis Cooper, and Nancy Mitford's Lady Leone.

Cecil Beaton described her as the most adulated beauty of her generation. "She has developed such force of personality that she blows everything superficial, tawdry, or false before her like a typhoon. She is tireless, indomitable, and courageous; frailer creatures fall by the way, but she has never lost the radiance and poise of someone who has always been greatly admired and loved." With regard to her sartorial prowess, he calls Lady Cooper "a day-dream dresser": "In matters of self-adornment she has always been an individualist and has never followed fashion. Instead of wearing the pink and white of a debutante, she dressed in stone colours;

By all reports, Lady Diana Cooper was that special combination of looks, wit, and insouciance which, though generally regarded as style, in truth has very little to do with fashion. Ever the actress, the indomitable Lady Cooper wove pearls through her hair to dramatize the wrapping and layering of her *Arabian Nights*—inspired costume. Pearls were consistent with her aristocratic upbringing, and she wore them constantly, whether dressed in a traditional picture hat and soft dress for day or in costume for a more creative occasion such as the opulent Beistegui Ball held in Venice in 1951.

wheat sheaves instead of roses decorated her hats. . . . A favourite combination of hers consisted of velvet slacks, three rows of pearls, a large but short fox fur cape, and a yachting cap."

In August 1936 Lady Cooper accompanied Wallis Simpson, another member of the "Corrupt Coterie," as it was sometimes called, on a trip in the Adriatic that fueled rumors of Wallis's affair with England's King Edward VIII. The romance, one of the great love stories of the century, resulted in the king's abdication of the throne, an act of devotion by Queen Mary's dapper son. The rather rough diamond of well-bred Baltimore ancestry on her mother's side and working-class roots on her father's side, Simpson became a busy international dignitary, organizing her and her husband's social schedule as if she were a queen and the duke her king. Freed of official state duties, the pair could select and choose the events they would grace with their presence, the dinners they would host, the parties they would attend, the friends and acquaintances they would visit, even the golf matches in which the duke would play—decisions made always with the couple's social aspirations firmly in mind. As part of her agenda of social advancement, Simpson's friend and mentor in Paris, the actress and prophetic decorator Elsie de Wolfe, refined Wallis's entertaining, socializing, home-decorating, and even dressing skills. Soon she and the duke were lauded as paragons of elegance.

The duke expressed his love for his duchess, whom he called "Your Highness," and his love of elegance through gifts of exquisite jewelry. According to Nicholas Rayner of Sotheby's, Geneva, the duke "had very good taste and spent an enormous amount of time and trouble choosing and commissioning jewels for the duchess." Many pieces commemorated important occasions, such as Simpson's fortieth birthday and their nuptials. Some of her most spectacular jewels include eighty-seven pieces from Cartier, their favorite jeweler, and twenty-three from Van Cleef and Arpels. Among these were the duchess's favorite bauble, a turquoise, amethyst, and diamond necklace; a charm bracelet of crosses, each representing a milestone in her life; and the diamond bracelet with an enormous sapphire-and-diamond clasp that she wore with her blue crêpe Mainbocher wedding dress.

As a peace offering in the wake of the duke's abdication, an act precipitated by his marriage to the twice-divorced American woman, Queen Mary gave her son a string of twenty-eight graduated natural pearls with a diamond clasp. In 1950 Cartier made the natural pearl pendant, and in 1964 the duke and duchess added a strand of twenty-nine cultured pearls—along with a stunning pair of Van Cleef and Arpels earrings made from one white and one black pearl, both surrounded by diamonds. The duchess wore the complete set to the duke's funeral in 1972. Photographs of the duchess at social events around the world attest to her fondness for pearls. In a spectacular bid of $1.4 million, American designer Calvin Klein bought the necklaces and the detachable drop, along with a diamond and gold "eternity" (it inspired his fragrance of the same name) ring, at Sotheby's in 1987, when the entire collection of Wallis's jewelry was sold at auction. The auction helped raise $50 million for l'Institut Pasteur and its AIDS research.

In 1987 Calvin and Kelly Klein shared one thing in common with the late Duke and Duchess of Windsor—pearls. Calvin bought the duchess's pearls for his wife as a romantic gesture. Taking a modern approach, Kelly is well known for having worn the collection of renowned pearls in Vogue with jeans. The duchess herself often wore the pair of necklaces au naturel.

Although the duchess set a trend for wearing smart little suits in the daytime and neat, covered-up evening clothes, detractors say she was too pristine. According to Eleanor Lambert, "She had to always be chic, chic, chic." Admirers like John Fairchild found her "impeccable, close to perfection in matters of fashion." The duchess herself, who learned about meticulous grooming from her grandmother, wrote in *Vogue* magazine, "I don't give much time to clothes, as mine are just correct, well-cut and of good materials, allowing me to wear them for several years. . . . Since I can't be pretty, I try to look sophisticated, but, unfortunately, I always want to be dressed like everybody else. . . . When I am out I always feel dowdy, and wish that I had thought of getting that dress, and wearing it that way." About her unobtrusive tailored style, the duchess wrote, "What you learn in your childhood about clothes stays with you all your life. I was rather poor and had to buy clothes that would do for the morning, for shopping, for the afternoon—practical, long-wearing, all-day dresses. I still buy that way. . . . The training of being poor is the most valuable one in the world—even if being poor doesn't last."

A compatriot of the duchess, Gertrude Vanderbilt Whitney, was born in America in 1875, and her life spanned an era of intense change, witnessing, for example, the emancipation of women, the rise of the American aristocracy, and the introduction of the new traditionalist. Photographs of her throughout much of her life reflect the vestiges of the Edwardian period, with its well-heeled, lacy style of dress, adorned with pearls wrapped about the neck and knotted at waist level.

Gertrude became a formidable force in New York society, as well as an accomplished sculptress whose statues grace Manhattan's landmark Central Park. "Uptown she was very regal. Downtown she was entirely different," observed her friend Jo Davidson. ". . . Gertrude's life became a struggle between these two people—the perfect lady in the House of Worth ball gown and the $600,000 Payne pearls [from her husband, Harry Payne Whitney's family], and the passionate bohemian in an exotic costume dancing barefoot in the moonlight."

Gertrude Vanderbilt, the daughter of Cornelius Vanderbilt II, married Harry Payne Whitney in 1896, and within the family, it is believed that these pearls were a wedding gift from Colonel Oliver Payne, Harry's uncle. Although they know that their own mother had the pearls at one point, Gertrude's granddaughters do not know what has happened to them. "People of my mother's generation had so much of everything that nobody kept track," explains one of the Long Island sisters. "This is the sadness. So many pearl necklaces were packed by a maid in New York and sent off to somewhere for vacation, then sent off to somewhere else. There were many, many houses, and many, many servants. Nobody took care of things. Each thought the other was looking after the pearls."

In this photograph by Baron Adolph de Meyer, Gertrude wears her pearl necklace with a costume by one of her favorite artists, Léon Bakst, who designed for Sergei Diaghilev's Ballets Russes and also greatly influenced Yves Saint-Laurent. A sculptor and patron of the arts, Gertrude founded the Whitney Museum of Modern Art in 1931.

Gertrude's mother, Alice, is also noted for her pearls, some of which ended up with Gertrude's soon-to-be sister-in-law, Gloria Morgan, mother of the present-day painter and fashion designer Gloria Vanderbilt. Morgan was having lunch at the Ambassador Hotel in New York with her fiancé Reggie Vanderbilt and his mother, Alice. Feeling warmly toward Gloria, since a recent test proved Ms. Morgan to be a virgin, Alice asked Reggie if Gloria had "received her pearls yet." When Reggie allowed that he couldn't afford the kind of pearls proper for his betrothed, his mother ordered the head waiter to bring her a pair of scissors. According to author Barbara Goldsmith, "She then removed the rope of pearls that wrapped twice around her neck and fell below her waist, cut off about one third, or $70,000 worth, and handed them to Gloria. 'There you are, Gloria,' she said. 'All Vanderbilt women have pearls.'"

The first woman to fly as a passenger over the Atlantic, and the first solo pilot to attempt the crossing, Amelia Earhart is a late-1920s and early-1930s role model for the new traditionalist. The prototype of the modern woman, Earhart was tall (five feet eight inches), lean (one hundred eighteen pounds), and athletic. In a description that both fits Earhart and rings surprisingly familiar today, *The New York Times* noted in 1931: "Any description of the ideal modern girl invariably specifies that she must be good at outdoor sports. A long stride, a strong arm, sunburned hair, a tanned complexion have come to be regarded as part of the picture of American beauty."

In 1933 Earhart licensed her name to a line of clothing. "I just don't like shopping very much," she revealed to one interviewer. "I hate ruffles, and at the price I could pay that was all I could buy. So I decided to design clothes. They are nothing exciting, just good lines and good materials for women who lead active lives." Like Marlene Dietrich and Katharine Hepburn, Earhart preferred the comfort and freedom of tailored trousers, and occasionally wore riding breeches, especially when flying. "I had no intention whatever of trying to set a fashion in transatlantic air attire," she protested, but her combination of high laced boots, brown breeches, a silk blouse with necktie and scarf, and a leather jacket came to define the public's notion of how a female aviator should dress. "I don't get all cluttered up for an automobile ride. Why should I dress any differently for all this?"

Earhart may not have intended to set a fashion trend, but her vigorous life, which foreshadowed the busy existences of today's modern traditionalists, called for practical, menswear-inspired clothing that presaged the rise of American sportswear. Earhart's

Amelia Earhart, captured in a softer moment away from the cockpit, but not without her signature pearls.

DREAM

concession to decoration was her use of silk scarves and pearls. One of the most recognizable photographs of Earhart is a close-up showing her in the cockpit with her helmet and goggles, fingering her double strand of pearls. On the ground pearls remained her identifying accessory too, for day and night. They softened her look, as they have done for many pioneering women.

A generation of traditionalists later, the *New York Times* reporter and editor Charlotte Curtis began as a society-page writer, fought for a tour of duty to cover the Vietnam War, and became the first woman to edit the paper's op-ed page and, as associate editor, the first of her gender to have her name grace its masthead. According to a review of a biography of Curtis in the *New York Observer,* "Her mocking voice as a society writer perfectly matched the leveling tendencies of the period, while her maidenly demeanor soothed the old guard. In her trademark strand of pearls [a four-strand necklace of sizable graduated pearls], Charlotte Curtis slipped almost undetected into positions of power. . . . Polite but persistent, she took the modest opportunities offered to her as a female reporter and shrewdly traded up, surpassing not only most of the women at the paper, but most of the men. Her sex did not hold her back for long. She had the zeitgeist on her side, as well, and there may be something to be said for a good strand of pearls."

In the arts sculptress Elizabeth Brim is yet another modern traditionalist whose anchor to time-honored values has given her a certain freedom to excel in a field in which few women have dared tread. She's a blacksmith. In 1985, while making jewelry for a class at Penland, the arts and crafts school in North Carolina, Brim's group needed to go to the blacksmith's shop to forge a special hammer. At midnight Brim still struggled with an unformed chunk of metal, long after her male classmates had gone home without so much as an offer of assistance. Overnight her mind raced with all the things she would make if she could process iron, and she went back to the shop the next day to tackle blacksmithing again. This time the men offered pointers, and Brim became the first woman to dedicate herself to the male-dominated craft. Her first sculpture was a pair of high-heeled steel shoes (which one admirer of her work later purchased as a wedding present for his wife), inspired by a fairy tale about twelve dancing princes. She went on to create high-heeled boudoir shoes sporting feathers made of forge-welded wire, and a tiara that rests ingeniously on a pillow of inflated steel.

"My mother didn't approve of my chosen medium, though," acknowledges Brim. "She said blacksmithing wasn't very ladylike." In response, a fellow student told

her, "Just wear a string of pearls and you will always be ladylike." Brim came back the next day sporting the sixteen-inch necklace of 3 mm pearls that she had won at a sporting goods store giveaway. "Now, I am quite the collector," she says, proudly pointing out that she has eighteen-, twenty-, twenty-four, and thirty-inch necklaces of much bigger pearls, two bracelets, and a variety of pearl earrings. "My ex-husband gave me the eighteen- and the twenty-four-inch ones and said, 'I don't want to catch you wearing these at the forge.' My mother gave me the longest one, and those are baroque pearls."

As Brim says, "I have to wear pearls now; they're something of a signature for me." Even her associates and students have caught on to the fashion. In 1998 during the first all-female session that Brim taught, one of the students gave every classmate a string of pearls. Several years earlier a visiting professor, blacksmith Doug Henderson, liked the idea of Brim's pearls so much that he went to the dime store during a lunch break and bought pearl necklaces for everyone in the class—male and female—including himself. "To give an idea of the impression it made, I should tell you that Doug is a great big typical blacksmith-looking guy who is totally bald and has an enormous bushy mustache; he is kind of prickly too," says Brim. His necklace was distinguished by a heart-shaped pearl dangling from the center.

In person, SoHo artist Michele Oka Doner possesses a sculptural presence not unlike her shimmering metalwork. Doner is distinguished for her artwork—such as the black terrazzo floor embedded with two thousand cast bronze starfish and other sea-inspired creatures, which stretches a half mile across the Miami International Airport. "I was always told that if I wanted to be a serious artist I would have to prove myself by leaving everything behind," she recalls. "That meant Shalimar and lipstick and the rest. But I am my mother's daughter, raised in Miami Beach. I have sailed on ocean liners and walked down the Champs-Élysées. I had no intention of giving up grooming and beautiful clothes. The decision *not* to give up these things freed me to be much more inventive, curiously enough," she explains, lamenting that women have given up their power of style. "Our mythology has changed," she insists. "Women don't think of themselves as mermaids and sirens anymore. Women like Jackie Kennedy and Grace Kelly did. They knew who they were. They used their tails. It is time we reclaim beauty."

For her fiftieth birthday Michele's husband wanted to give her a pearl-and-diamond necklace. Michele preferred pearls by themselves, because she wanted something she could wear every day. "I saw Helena Rubenstein's pearls at auction

years ago, and there was a synergy operating there between the two strands, and I saw a beautiful pattern—a rich negative space, as happens between the leaves of a tree— as if the pearls were communicating with one another." With her memory, aided by the auction catalog, Michele set out to learn about pearls and find the perfect neck- lace. She accomplished both, with the help of Salvador Assael, the man who pro- moted black pearls and encouraged the current boom in the South Sea pearl business. Michele ended up with two necklaces, matched in color and size: one semibaroque strand and a string of off-round pearls. Michele likes the opales- cence of the baroque pearls and the way the light and negative space of the neck- laces play off each other.

"Kitty Hawks and I had a diamonds-and-pearls lunch at Le Cirque. We talked about work and ceramics, which she loves, and all that we were doing. And I was noticing that Kitty is also someone who has aged fabulously—she has beautiful gray hair—and is not afraid of aging. It is as if there is a new tribe of women who are blessing their lives instead of detracting from them. We gave ourselves permission to be fifty. She can wear her diamond ring every day, and I can wear my pearls. In your forties you don't think like that. Words like 'matri- arch' were negative and now they are positive. Gray hair was once negative and now is more positive. It is part of a reassessing. No, it is more than that. It is a tremendous inversion of values."

Doner's comment brings the discussion of traditionalists full circle. The artist and her contemporaries, working in fields as disparate as market forecasting, fashion design, philanthropy, and journalism, are indeed engaged in a reassessment of values. They are carving out a new identity where they can embrace the venerable traditions of their past while enjoying the freedoms of the new millennium. In part, their path has been cleared by the steady march of earlier generations of pioneering women. But in order to clear a path, some things must be sacrificed. These new traditionalists are experimenting to dis-

Transplanted from Miami, where the airport floor is inlaid with her golden sea motif, New York sculptress Michele Oka Doner, photographed by Sheila Metzner, is a work of art in her birthday pearls.

cover what they will save and what they will forgo in order to create the delicate balance of order and stability that is so appealing during times of change. The era of the American aristocracy, which both proscribed and privileged the lives of some of the women in this chapter, is a fading memory; and a "new tribe of women," to use Doner's term, is at the helm of contemporary society, poised to redefine the traditions that make us modern.

*&*earls are the badge of innocence, yet they are the wild cards of fantasies. Yes, even pearls can step out of their traditional milieu and into a highly individual, idiosyncratic vision that shows off the gem's rich versatility and contradictory nature. Depending on how they are employed, pearls can convey chastity and modesty or opulence and sensuality.

With a chestful of these myth-laden gems, a woman can pose as any intriguing personality, from a renowned marchioness to a grand courtesan. A man can masquerade as an Indian potentate or assume the guise of a costume-ball chimera

MAKERS

or myriad characters from stage and screen. In *The Young Rajah* (1939), for example, Rudolph Valentino was nearly upstaged by the quantity of pearls on his maharaja's costumes. Artist and set designer Erté covered his own Arabian getup with pearls for special occasions, and Sir Cecil Beaton used pearl dresses to add visual texture, wit, and surprise to a remarkable self-portrait, and again to encase his close friend, Stephen Tennant, in another photographic reverie.

Honing their skills in the social arts, the decorative arts, film, and the performing arts, the people in this chapter—the Dream Makers whose passions have taken them outside the boundaries of traditional society, conventional morality, or even gender roles—have stretched the limits of their creative potentials and, in the process, showed the many facets of human experience.

Coco Chanel (née Gabrielle Chanel, 1883–1971) rose from humble origins to become a practical Dream Maker—a design and business visionary who in 1908 began a fashion dynasty by making hats. She then opened her first shop at number 21 Rue Cambon, in Paris (in 1921 she moved it to number 31, where it remains today). By the time she opened her shop for millinery and clothing in the northern French resort of Deauville, in 1913, and her *maison de couture* in the southwestern French resort Biarritz, in 1915, the Chanel revolution was well under way. She not only dreamed of fashions that would liberate women from the body-constraining, even disfiguring, styles

PAGE 112: *Marlene* Dietrich as a jewel thief in *Desire* (1936).
LEFT: The Honorable Stephen Tennant, the reclusive but charming and witty author, poet, and painter, was Cecil Beaton's friend, mentor, and frequent model. For this photo by Beaton, he poses as Prince Charming, in a costume laden with pearls. Tennant's mother is wearing ropes of pearls around her neck in John Singer Sargent's acclaimed portrait of *The Wyndham Sisters*.
RIGHT: Rudolph Valentino also dons the iridescent gems for his leading role in *The Young Rajah* (1922). Even covered in pearls from turban to toes, the first silver screen heartthrob maintains his manly appeal.

From delicate single-strand choker with gemstone drop to hip-grazing rope, pearls were a favorite accessory in Lillie Langtry's personal wardrobe. Here pearls festoon the bosom of her costume by Worth for her role as Mrs. Trevelyan in the semibiographical play called *The Degenerates*, which premiered in London in August 1899. A humble girl from Jersey, who became the first socialite to take up a career as an actress, Langtry was renowned both for her beauty and for her choice of husbands and lovers, among them King Edward VII. The king's wife, Alexandra, actually liked and befriended the determined and independent Langtry.

of the past, she eventually wanted the world to imitate and paraphrase her message. Chanel knew that imitations of her fashions would never be as luxurious as her originals, but her message was designed to radiate beyond the narrow elite world of her private clientele to reach every woman, everywhere.

Chanel's iconoclastic approach forever altered the foundation of women's apparel. Her brand of glamour enlisted practical fabrics, such as wool jersey and tweed, in shapes that suggested the female shape underneath but were ultimately wearable and comfortable. Chanel's use of classically female emblems, such as bows, flowers, and fragrance, incorporated the same kind of down-to-earth thinking. When it came to jewelry, the feisty French couturiere would be the first to understand the mass appeal of making a statement with bold costume jewelry mixed with real jewels. In a time when fine jewelry was a measure of wealth, Coco blurred the lines between faux and the real thing, making certain that the accessory was the jewelry, not its price tag.

A woman needs ropes and ropes of pearls," said Coco Chanel. And people listened. White pearls, natural and faux, cascading over a black top were as much a Chanel signature as her interlocking Cs. She often mixed real gems with her costume jewelry, and eventually, even she could not tell the difference.

Here she is with her friend Serge Lifar of the Ballets Russes. While Mademoiselle Chanel only wore pants in the country, she was never without her pearls. Coco's insistence on the constant presence of pearls, even with pants, began to take form early in her career when she wrapped the gems around her neck to go horseback riding with one of her first lovers and confidants, the duke of Westminster.

LEFT: Karl Lagerfeld's ode to Coco's everlasting spirit from the runway of the spring-summer 1995 ready-to-wear collection.

Pearls were an extension of Chanel's personality. She liked their understatement and their subtle glamour. The diminutive Mademoiselle Chanel covered herself in pearls, finding it more attractive to drape longer ropes at least twice around the neck than to wear shorter necklaces in multiples. "If there is jewelry, there must be a lot," she proclaimed. "If it's real, that's showy and in bad taste. The jewelry I make is very fake and very beautiful. Even more beautiful than the real thing." Ever the businesswoman, she liked the fact that all the aristocrats and royal ladies of her day wore pearls. It meant that her fake ones had a built-in cachet for women everywhere.

Chanel could not imagine a dress or suit without accessories. "Accessories are what make or mark a woman," she claimed. Despite the fact that an older contemporary of Chanel's, French designer Paul Poiret, was the first to use costume jewelry in his collections, Chanel instituted her glass pearls and colorful *pâte de verre* gems as integral to her look. With the help of her friend the talented jewelry designer Count Fulco di Verdura, Chanel created her collection of multicolored beads, crosses, and other bold Renaissance-inspired jewelry, the success of which helped Chanel legitimize costume jewelry.

"Coco was great for costume jewelry—chains and the sort," says James Brady, columnist, author, and former publisher of *Women's Wear Daily*. Chanel and Brady were close friends during the last ten years of the designer's life. "I have a photo of her on my wall in East Hampton that she gave me," says Jim. "She looks terribly correct," he continues, describing the black dress and white jacket of her own design that she wears and the ubiquitous cigarette in her hand. "Around her neck she has a couple of her familiar chains, and she also has a couple strands of what appear to be poppits," he chortles. Brady's note of irreverence is nonetheless apropos. Poppits were inexpensive molded plastic beads that resembled oversized pearls and came in a variety of colors. Sold in strands, poppits could be lengthened or shortened by snapping them apart. The nonchalance of poppits is in keeping with the look Chanel established during the 1920s when she looped long ropes of natural and faux pearls around her neck to wear with her tweed suits, little black dresses, or trousers and sweaters for weekends in the country.

Chanel's first pearl necklace was a gift from her lover, friend, and lifelong influence Boy Capel, who made his fortune in the coal-importing business in France. The jewels were an attempt to assuage his beloved mistress who complained one day that she had never received the obligatory flowers and jewels from him. The

A relaxed sweater jacket, on Milla Jovovich, for the Chanel spring-summer 1998 couture collection, worn with lots and lots of cultured pearls and other designs from the Chanel Fine Jewelry collection.

next day Capel arranged for a delivery of flowers every half hour, all day long. The following day he asked Cartier to deliver a jewel. In jest, he had ordered a tiara for his queen, which Chanel rejected because she said it fit neither her wrist nor her neck. The tiara was promptly exchanged for a more practical strand of pearls, which Chanel wore constantly.

When traveling, Chanel carried all her jewels in a nondescript small brown canvas bag. She admitted that nothing was insured—insurance was, too high to be possible.

In *Coco Chanel: Her Life, Her Secrets* her friend Marcel Haedrich quotes several of Chanel's famous comments about jewelry, which offer succinct insight into her philosophy: "I'm covered with chokers, necklaces, brooches, earrings, stones of every color, so many that no one understands me when I say I don't like jewels," she said. "What I don't like is a stone for the stone's own sake, the headlight diamond, the eye-gouger that stands as an identification, an outward sign of wealth for the husband or the lover of the woman wearing it. Nor do I like jewelry for jewelry's sake—the diamond clip, the quote-string-of-pearls-unquote that one takes out of the safe for evening display, that one puts back in the safe after dinner and that probably belongs to a corporation. That's all jewelry-to-be-sold-in-case-of-emergency. Jewelry for the rich. I don't like it." Chanel believed that "in the street one should wear only fakes. One wears real jewelry at home, for one's own enjoyment, now and then." Chanel also noted: "I made false pearls in order not to have to wear my own. I was told I looked pretty with them. I said to myself, 'All women ought to be able to wear them to improve their looks.'"

In summary, Brady offers this: "Chanel always said that if you notice the dress and not the woman, that is a fashion mistake. You must notice the woman first; it is the same with jewelry. I think that pearls are understated and slightly reticent, and for that reason they really are very effective."

If Coco Chanel dreamed of a relaxed modern style that any woman could enjoy, Diana Vreeland (1906–1989) was her creative antithesis. Of equal influence, Diana's strengths lay not in business and profits, as Chanel's did, but in her ability to cater to the American woman's higher, more refined fashion instincts. Instead of lowering aesthetic standards, Diana raised them and translated women's unspoken longing for imaginative guidance into creative visuals that appeared in two of the world's most powerful fashion magazines and in inspirational style exhibits at New York's largest art museum.

Diana Vreeland in ivory and pearls. Photographed by Evelyn Hofer.

Her first job, at age thirty-three, was as author of the "Why Don't You" column for *Harper's Bazaar,* in which she offered quirky society news as well as imaginative fashion tips, such as advising her readers to buy shoes in pairs and put rubber soles onto one pair for use on rainy days. As a fashion editor at *Bazaar* and as editor in chief during her tenure at *Vogue,* Vreeland created as many trends as those she reported. She orchestrated bold editorial photographs of fashions, such as one that spotlighted Yves Saint-Laurent's 1963 thigh-high crocodile boots or one featuring a black-painted hand holding a giant marquise diamond from Harry Winston. She promoted original American designers and created the fashion for specific styles like the turtleneck sweater. Diana discovered early supermodels, such as Twiggy, the symbol of the 1960s with her owl-like black eye makeup and thin, androgynous figure; the leggy Verushka, whom Diana daringly showed photographed in the nude; and Lauren Hutton, with the now famous gap between her two front teeth. At the Metropolitan Museum of Art Diana revived the faltering Costume Institute and created precedent-setting lifestyle and fashion exhibits about everything from Russian dress and Diaghilev's Ballets Russes to dance clothes, riding clothes, Hollywood costumes, and women who epitomized American style.

As icons, Diana and Coco were their own best representatives. Coco advertised her approach to fashion better than anyone else. Diana unveiled her individuality through her work and her own quirky and exotic appearance, as well as through her renowned dinner parties, which were filled with regal guests from international artistic and social communities.

Coco and Diana also loved and gained strength from the men in their lives. Even though Chanel never married, she had notorious love affairs. Russia's Grand Duke Dimitri gave her a strand of historic Romanov pearls and inspired her sense of luxury. The duke of Westminster provided her with her own fabric mill, and his wardrobe inspired Chanel's use of country tweeds, trousers, and sweaters. Iribe, the celebrated illustrator, helped Chanel create an extravagant exhibition of diamond designs.

In contrast to Coco, Diana had been exposed to grandeur and sophistication from an early age, living a salon life with her family in England and France, and preferred a more settled lifestyle with her husband and children. Diana wrote in her biography, that her husband, Reed Vreeland, possessed "fantastic glamour," and that she remained a bit shy in his presence, even after forty years of marriage.

In true Dream Maker fashion, both Coco and Diana are still famed for their propensity to elaborate on the facts of their lives to suit their fantasies of the moment:

When Diana told the story of her youth and the influences on her sense of self, she frequently added a new association, a different name, a "favorite" adventure; and Chanel often recast the abandonment and poverty of her youth and hedged about her early beginnings as a courtesan. Both visionaries spoke in oft-quoted maxims, to define style philosophies that helped to explain the changes in fashion in the twentieth century. Two of Vreeland's axioms reveal the underpinnings of her dream-making posture: "Elegance is refusal" and "Never fear being vulgar, just boring." Chanel bequeathed to Diana, as a memento of friendship and respect, a black velvet bag containing the natural pearl earrings that the designer always wore. "Actually, on the day she died," Diana wrote, "as far as we know, her *great* collection of jewels, including the famous Romanov pearls Dimitri had given her, disappeared *off the face of the earth.*"

"I went to school and had a fine education, but I learned everything I knew from Diana," says Laura Clark, who was one of Diana's editorial protégées at *The Bazaar* (as staffers used to refer to *Harper's Bazaar*). "When I arrived, I was dressed from the boys' department at Brooks Brothers. I also had a boy's tuxedo that I wore at night, with big pearl earrings; Diana loved it." Diana instructed her to build a wardrobe by starting with one "perfect suit," Laura recalls. "She recommended a gray one from Pauline Potter [later Mrs. Philippe de Rothschild] who was pioneering the concept of ready-to-wear at Hattie Carnegie, even if I had to pay for it over time." In essence, Diana taught Laura "to find a look and stay with it, including one hairdo, one lipstick"—and to be herself, because "life would really be so much easier."

According to Clark, Vreeland had a wicked sense of humor. "I'll never forget the first time she had a meeting with all of us at *The Bazaar*. She made a grand entrance—wearing a turban, waving her cigarette holder, staggering under the weight of the pearls dripping down her suit. Then she announced, in all seriousness, 'My girls, I want you to know that simplicity is the thing.'

"Diana loved pearls," Clark continues. "Every day for a couple of years she wore little pearl earrings with a fake canary diamond dangling off of each one. One evening, she took a necklace that had begun to bore her and twisted it around her wrist. It was sort of looping and draping around all through dinner. It was marvelous. I tried it right away and felt very glamorous. I couldn't stop waving my hand around.

"Diana put pearls in the magazine in the 1950s and made them come back in fashion. We'd bring sapphires for some of the photo shoots. She would say that sapphires looked like chewing gum in black-and-white pictures and would tell us to bring diamonds and pearls." About her own experience with Diana and pearls, Clark recalls: "The first time I went to Paris, I bought this navy-blue sequined dinner suit with a short skirt and fitted jacket. I was thrilled. Diana said, 'My dear, the only thing you can wear with that is pearls.' She also told me to wear blue mascara and just pile it on for night, along with a little lip gloss, and then stick my head up and walk into a place as if I owned it."

There were other strong voices of fashion who blossomed during the period between the Great Wars, a time when creativity exploded. Coco and Diana were surrounded by fresh thinkers such as couturiers Vionnet and Elsa Schiaparelli. Vionnet was a master technician who created bias-cut dresses, the cowl neck, the halter neckline, and wrap coats in soft, sinewy fabrics. Italian-born Schiaparelli lived with her husband in New York and Boston before settling in Paris in 1922. She defined the shape of clothing with her wide-shouldered pagoda sleeve, from 1933 until Christian Dior's New Look in 1947. The irreverent designer loved humor and the whimsy of things like dyed fur and exposed zippers. She was greatly influenced by the Cubist and Surrealist movements and hired such artists as Salvador Dali, Jean Cocteau, and Christian Bérard to design fabrics and Jean Schlumberger to create jewelry. Her penchant for the irreverant and outrageous was evident in her introduction of shocking pink as a signature color and her use of such items as buttons in the shape of acrobats, music-box handbags, and Dali's high-heeled-shoe hat.

The new thinking during the 1920s and early 1930s influenced writers, dancers, dramatists, and artists who railed against the rigid controls of the past and the empty excesses of the Edwardians. There was a loosening of moral boundaries, a relaxation of restricting fashions, and an almost childish delight in the freedom of imagination that the era fostered. This intellectually fertile atmosphere opened the door for two divergent talents: the American cabaret entertainer Josephine Baker and the illustrator and designer Erté, both of whom aimed to inspire.

Prior to her arrival in Paris, Josephine Baker had been an enormous success in the United States in a review called *Chocolate Dandies.* In her revealing costumes, often made of only feathers and pearls, Baker was the *enfant terrible* of Paris as the star of *La Revue Nègre.* "When Josephine slithered off the tree on the stage of the Folies-Bergère and

Starting in 1933, Jeanne Toussaint presided over Cartier's *haute joaillerie.* Nicknamed "the Panther"—she was fascinated with the cats—Ms. Toussaint was not specifically a jewelry designer, but a foolproof barometer for style, invested with a discretion that was totally trusted by her lover, Louis Cartier.

And what did this woman of legendary taste wear around her neck? Pearls, of course. As many as five long strands of pearls the size of chickpeas, which hung well below her rib cage. Often she would modify the strands by constricting a section with her favorite brooch. This addition created a chokerlike effect and left a cascade of pearls which Ms. Toussaint let fall forward over one shoulder.

began dancing, wearing only the famous banana-belt costume and shells around her neck for 'La Danse de Sauvage,' everything went on except penetration," says her son, New York restaurateur Jean-Claude Baker. "The bananas looked positively phallic all around her, and she was moving her behind. Half of the people were horrified; the other half were excited. After the performance Gertrude Stein, Jean Cocteau, and Picasso screamed and declared a new style was born.

"Josephine had no complex about being scandalously naked onstage, in any of her costumes, because she knew she could do it forcefully and gracefully," Jean-Claude explains. "She was a free spirit and a great actress. She was also outrageous and knew what people expected of her."

The rebellious side of the woman known for parading down the Champs-Élysées with her pet cheetah, or for having once taken a gorilla as her constant com-

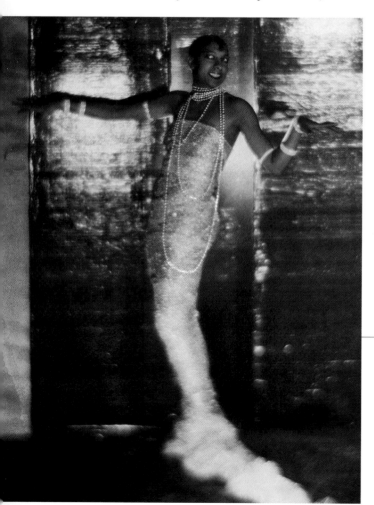

panion, gave way to the loving, nurturing side of her personality when Josephine the dancer teamed with Josephine the Universal Mother to fulfill another dream. Using her fame as a successful black entertainer, Josephine began to address the issue of racial equality and unity. In addition to her vocal stance, over time she adopted a total of twelve children of all races and nationalities. She was fifty years old by the time she had opened her home to the first six. Josephine turned her country château in Périgord, called Les Milandes, into "the Capital of Universal Brotherhood" for her "rainbow tribe."

The racy Josephine Baker makes a glamorous statement in her skintight costume and showering of pearls. OPPOSITE: Erté frequently used large amounts of pearls in his glamorous designs. Here, he covered himself with imitation pearls for an evening in Monte Carlo in 1922.

Near the end of Josephine's life, in 1973, Jean-Claude accompanied his mother on a trip from Paris to New York. By then Josephine had spent much of her wealth, but she had not lost her interest in jewels. "We went to the duty-free shop where they had lots of fake jewels," says Jean-Claude. "I was a star in Germany by that time and making a lot of money singing in a club, and I wanted to buy the biggest ones for Josephine. She said that since everyone knew she had owned the most beautiful jewels, they would know these big ones were fake. I bought her a bunch. As long as they were not oversized, they were acceptable. The collection included a parure of ruby jewelry surrounded by pearls—a pendant, earrings, and a brooch. On Josephine, it looked real."

For Josephine Baker, the chasteness of pearls was exotic and extravagant. . The luminous spheres were also sexy and became her signature, encircling her neck,

wrapped around her wrists and ankles, or draped over her body. Many of her most memorable costumes were made with pearls. Sometimes pearls covered very skimpy shorts or were strung into a halter neck to hold up the costume. Another outfit featured large, Indian-style fan-shaped pearl earrings and a feathered loincloth. For a more sedate performance, pearls completely encrusted a long mermaid dress. The classic Hoyningen-Huene photograph of a statuesque Josephine, naked, holding a waterfall of pearls that reach from her chin to her toes, is an everlasting image of the popular entertainer.

Erté, the St. Petersburg–born illustrator and designer, created some of the costumes and sets for glamorous nightclubs and cabarets such as the Folies-Bergère, Bal Tabarin, Teatre Femina, and the Ziegfeld Follies. Like Josephine Baker, he celebrated the female form. While Baker's reverence was more earthy in her role as a sex goddess,

Erté applied his reverie to illustration and the decorative arts, creating some of the most feminine drawings of the twentieth century. While he wasn't a fashion designer, the female form, clothes, jewels, flowers, hats, scarfs, and lots of pearls are characteristic themes of his heavily detailed and fanciful drawings. Erté applied his aesthetic to all of his crafts, whether he was dressing a dancer, a stage, or a cover for *Harper's Bazaar* (which he illustrated for twenty-two years, from 1915 to 1937), or outfitting himself.

Erté, whose name comes from the French pronunciation of his initials, R.T. (which stand for Romain de Tirtoff), had very strong opinions about men and women and the way they dress. He found men's clothing stiff and uninspired, and favored softly tailored outfits turned out in silk and satin. Occasionally he would entertain his dinner guests and wear five antique Chinese kimonos, one over the other, and peel off a layer with each course of the meal. An aesthete, Erté frequently accessorized his beautifully tailored English suits with a small pearl bracelet and a diamond pinky ring.

About women, the designer claimed: "How many women could be beautiful. . . . If they would impartially analyze their defects as well as their advantages. . . . No woman is irredeemably 'ordinary.' Introduce some sort of harmony into the line of her clothes, her hairstyle, her make-up, all the little details of her toilette and her grooming, and the woman who for years you have thought of as 'ordinary' will become a revelation to you. . . . It is necessary to accentuate all one's physical qualities; as for defects, there are two possibilities: They can be disguised as well as possible, or, on the contrary, they can be exaggerated in such a way as to create a very personal style."

Erté credits his mother for his love of "all things connected with beautiful clothes and elegance." He credits the Indian and Persian miniatures that he found in his father's library for providing the initial source of his artistic style: their depiction of exotic female eyes with exaggerated eyebrows fascinated the young Erté. Much later, he also drew inspiration from the stylized illustrations of the English artist Aubrey Beardsley. With these deep-seated visions, Erté's drawings, fashions, costumes, and even some of his stage sets were graceful, sometimes whimsical, and always grounded in fantasy and reverie. The curving forms of his alphabet drawings, the arch of a stage set, the billowy leg of an Eastern costume were often covered with pearls. The soft, sensuous contours of a pearl and the dreamlike opalescence of these moonstruck gems made them obvious adornments for Erté's curvilinear images.

The sensuousness of pearls was a favorite theme for another pearl-loving contemporary of Baker's and Erté's, the author known simply as Colette. In a twist

on convention, Colette turned pearls into erotic bedroom toys for Chéri, the young male lover of the heroine, Léa, in *The Last of Chéri*. Chéri likes to roll his lover's pearls on the bed and twist them in his hands. When he undresses, revealing Léa's pearls around his neck, she is aroused at the sight of the luminescent gems against his skin: "He unbuttoned his pajamas, displaying a hard, darkish chest, curved like a shield; and the whites of his dark eyes, his teeth, and the pearls of the necklace gleamed in the over-all rosy glow of the room." Throughout the story the author illustrates that pearls are as potent for men as they are for women.

At home with pearls is a young Colette, the French novelist and performer (1873–1954) who cherished the beauty and the sensuous qualities that pearls possess.

How can pearls be so virginal and so decadent at the same time? Some of the most unforgettable answers can be found in Hollywood. *Some Like It Hot* (1959), one of the funniest and most ironic screen gems, features Jack Lemmon and Tony Curtis. Their comedic performances in female drag upstaged Marilyn Monroe, and as visual parody, their long pearl ropes and lace dresses pretty much say it all. Pearls offer the subtle authenticity that these men needed to pose as girls, a nuance that no other jewelry could provide.

Pearls have long been the staple of costume designers and actors for some of the silver screen's most memorable moments. For moviegoers, pearls have been synonymous with the elegance, glamour, and basic femininity of some of our favorite heroines. Miss Scarlet donned a triple strand of pearls for her marriage to Ashley in *Gone With the Wind* (1939). As the tragic heroine of *Sunset Boulevard* (1950), Gloria Swanson wore multiple strands of pearls twisted around her neck. Katharine Hepburn coiled pearls around the scarf she drapes around her neck and lets flow down her back in *Summertime* (1955). A single strand of pearls stands as a lasting image of Grace Kelly in *The Swan* (1956), which was the last film Grace made before she assumed her real-life role as princess of Monaco.

Very human and representative of a young American woman's fantasy, however inflated, is Audrey Hepburn's role in *Breakfast at Tiffany's* as Holly Golightly, a struggling young girl who comes to New York to marry her fortune. Paris couturier Hubert de Givenchy dressed Ms. Hepburn for the film (as he did in real life). For the opening scene, when Ms. Golightly has her

Marilyn "Sugar Kane" Monroe with her pearl-bedecked co-stars Jack Lemmon and Tony Curtis in Some Like It Hot. Billy Wilder's 1950s comedy won an Oscar for the pearly costumes.
OPPOSITE: *Marilyn coils pearls round the neckline of her dress and adds more MM glamour with pearl-drop earrings.*

coffee-and-a-roll breakfast and dreamfest gazing into Tiffany's windows, she wears a simple black skimmer. Since Holly lives on a shoestring, her predictable accessory would be a simple pearl necklace. But tapping into her rich-girl fantasy, Holly takes pearls to a more dramatic extreme and glamorizes her little black dress as if she were a queen. She starts with five strands of oversized pearls interspersed with rhinestones for coquettish sparkle, draping them over her head so that they slip down her back and her chest. As if her mélange weren't enough, she plants an oversized gemstone brooch over the closure, which Holly has turned to the front. Of course, Holly's eye-popping gems are frankly fake.

Perhaps Holly Golightly drew her inspiration from the pearl necklaces in Christian Dior's collection, or from other popular costume jewelers of the later 1950s. The owner of the New York costume jewelry company known as Miriam Haskell says that his company made pearls just like Ms. Golightly's, but doesn't have the records to substantiate his hunch that her pearls were Haskell's. The current owner of Trabert and Hoeffer jewelers, who provided a lot of Hollywood's glamorous jewelry, also recognizes the necklace as typical of their designs at that time, but the origins of Holly's illustrious bijoux remain a mystery.

The lasting importance of Holly Golightly's jewelry is that it adroitly used giant pearls to symbolize the deep human yearning for a bolder, more glamorous existence. "In the 1930s and the 1940s nobody made fine jewelry that was dramatic. It was almost all small," says Joan Castle Joseff, wife of the late Joseff of Hollywood, who made what Joan calls "movie jewelry." "The screen was bigger than life, and the jewelry had to be too," explains Joan. "When I used to take our jewelry around to the movie studios, I always hoped the director and the producers wouldn't get involved in the choices. They were constantly looking for little tiny things, because that was what their wives wore. We wanted to go directly to the designer or the star, because they always wanted dramatic pieces—jewelry with a presence. Joseff would always say, 'If you are going to wear jewelry, make a statement.'

"I used to say that pearls were only for weddings and graduations—and Jackie Onassis," she continues. "She certainly made them very popular. I don't know why, but now I wear them. They have to be big. And I love black pearls; just a single strand, about 10 mm in size, with a little ornament on the bottom. Mine are real; I wear them all the time."

Audrey Hepburn as the unforgettable Holly Golightly in *Breakfast at Tiffany's.*

Joseff made the seven-strand pearl necklace with ruby inserts that Bette Davis wore for her portrayal of the pearl-obsessed Queen Elizabeth I in *The Private Lives of Elizabeth and Essex* (1939), also known as *Elizabeth the Queen.* "Tyrone Power wore the same necklace when he portrayed a maharaja in *The Rains Came*, later in 1939," Joan notes, laughing, "and some people thought it looked better on him."

Joan tells another pearl story about movie idol and heartthrob, Errol Flynn. "We made a pearl stud earring for him for his role in *The Adventures of Don Juan* (1948). The studio was constantly calling for replacement earrings. We ended up making twenty-two in all. Flynn was apparently living up to the character's reputation during the filming. Every time he took one of those gals into his dressing room, she probably got one of our earrings."

Natasha Rambova, the formidable Hollywood art director during the 1920s, known as much for her studied sets and costumes as for her stormy marriage to the handsome actor Rudolph Valentino, made very climactic use of pearls. When the actress Alla Nazimova donned a wig of vibrating white baubles for the 1922 film version of Oscar Wilde's *Salome,* she became the surreal embodiment of Rambova's absolute creative vision, evincing the mutability of pearls. Basing her costumes on the fanciful, often erotic, and controversial drawings that British artist and illustrator Aubrey Beardsley had

R&B singer Mary J. Blige adds texture and drama to a simple slip dress with a sleek headdress that is sprinkled with seed pearls.
RIGHT: Alla Nazimova cut a wide swath through the theater and the nascent film industry at the turn of the century. The Russian-born actress, writer, film editor, and producer seemingly never stopped re-creating—and pushing— herself, taking on a new career in silent film at the age of 32 (1916). The head of Nazimova Productions, she is credited as producer on six films in five years, including *Salome* (1923), based on a play by Oscar Wilde. Here, with pearls as big as bubbles defining her headdress, she assumes the role of the film's title character.

rendered for a production of the play in 1893, Rambova worked her own alchemy to bring the illustrations to life on the screen. Soldiers wore black leotards and, around their necks, pearls the size of Ping-Pong balls. For the Dance of the Seven Veils, rather than using the diaphanous, pearl-trimmed gown and veiled headdress inspired by Beardsley's art, Rambova bowed to Nazimova's wish to show off her shapely curves. Nazimova dances before her stepfather in a

rubberized metallic minidress, a feather-and-pearl headdress, and fluttering wings of pearls that stretch out under her arms.

For his role in *The Young Rajah*, Natasha dressed her lover and future husband, Rudolph Valentino, in scandalously revealing swim trunks or little more than strings of pearls. Filmgoers thrilled to see the matinee idol's exposed flesh—the backdrop to pearls that spilled down his legs, wrapped about his ankles, and crisscrossed

his chest. Even his ears and his helmet dripped with the iridescent gems. Skimpy or not, the only costume Rambova preferred to see on her paramour was none at all. She insisted he looked best when he was nude.

Valentino's rajah wore more than one pearl costume. In a more covered-up look, his suit and shoes were encrusted with pearls. More than a dozen strands encircled his neck, ropes of the lustrous beads cascaded down his chest, and a clutch of pearl-covered rods anchored his turban like a sheaf of wheat. The film was a critical flop; however, it still generated moderate revenues.

While earlier films displayed pearls in idiosyncratic fashion, they were usually based on some example of historic splendor. In the turbulent 1960s and 1970s, however, movie pearls appeared in remarkable fashions. For his role as a rather dark transvestite, Tim Curry wore a choker of enormous white specimens in the cult classic *The Rocky Horror Picture Show* (1975). Big white pearls, dramatic face paint, and a big tattoo— all on a man wearing fishnet stockings—made a striking contrast. While she wasn't using pearls to magnify a sexual, gender statement, British costume designer Jocelyn Rickards draped a long rope of "fingernail-sized, maybe bigger" pearls to exaggerate model Peggy Moffat's dramatic peacock costume for a sequence in Michelangelo Antonioni's definitive fashion parody, *Blow-Up* (1966). Peggy symbolized 1960s style with her smoky eye makeup and her radically short, angular haircut by London's mod hairdresser Vidal Sasson. "Peggy's was an extraordinary costume," says Rickards. "I found the material in the Paris flea market—pure peacock colors.

*S*igourney Weaver is framed by long black gloves that are outlined with pearls in this graphic portrait by Robert Mapplethorpe.

BELOW: Costumer Trisha Biggar draped Natalie Portman in a fringe of pearls for her role as Queen Amidala in *Star Wars: Episode I: The Phantom Menace* (1999). The delicate strings of freshwater seed pearls "started life as an Edwardian veiling or sash for a dress," says Biggar. "There are forty or fifty strands of pearls and each is about forty inches long. I like the reflected light of pearls and the mystery of her face coming through the fringe. There is an innocence about pearls, and we often think of pearls as a young woman's decoration. Queen Amidala had purity and innocence, and pearls let us portray a lot of subtle ideas about her character."

PAGE 142: In this photo by Mick Rock, Tim Curry is immortalized in his jumbo pearls and eerie makeup for the kinky British horror-film spoof and cult classic *The Rocky Horror Picture Show* (1975).

PAGE 143: Alice Springs' study of jewelry designer Billy Boy, in Schiaparelli's own monkey-fur coat, a Schiaparelli hat, and vintage Chanel costume pearls, during his Paris period.

$\mathcal{B}$eginning in 1967, Bob Mackie created and produced close to fifty costumes every week during the eleven-year run of *The Carol Burnett Show*. Here, one of her wickedly funny costumes for her parody of Nora Desmond (Gloria Swanson) in *Sunset Boulevard*. Mackie exaggerates the waggish look of her dress and floppy boobs (made of rice) by adding a string of pearls all the way down the front and around the neck, pearl-and-rhinestone brooches, and giant pearl and rhinestone drop earrings. Mackie has used pearls for every type of design, from his costumes for Cher to the embroidery on his 1992 dress for Empress Bride Barbie.

"I had the dress reembroidered with peacock feathers, and we gave her a skullcap with peacock feathers sprouting at the top. On top of all the smoldering color, she had a very long strand of pearls that went two or three times around her neck and then down to her knees. I found it the most enjoyable film I'd ever made," Rickards concludes.

The renowned costume designer doesn't hesitate to volunteer her thoughts about pearls: "I love pearls. I love to run my fingers through them. In films I always use them for people in whom I want to display some kind of class. People who never put a foot wrong in what they wear. Somebody with perfect taste." Jocelyn admires women who wear baroque pearls and thinks that the irregularly shaped gems are chic, and she likes combinations, such as crystals and pearls with moonstones, where gems are the same color. "Barbara Hutton had an enormous flowered necklace like that," says Rickards. "I'd like to see a bathing suit all covered with pearls. It would look so marvelous in the water."

In recent years pearls have enjoyed a resurgence on the screen. In *The First Wives Club* (1996), Goldie Hawn, Bette Midler, and Diane Keaton portray very different characters whose matching pearl necklaces, given to one another as college graduation presents, are worn throughout the film as reminders of their shared histories. Kristin Scott-Thomas wore a magnificent double-strand necklace that danced across her bosom as she waltzed with Ralph Fiennes in *The English Patient* (1997). Costumer Aude Bronson-Howard slipped pearls around the neck of Claire Forlani for her role as the dutiful, traditional, and well-mannered daughter in *Meet Joe Black* (1998). Bronson-Howard explains the art of her job as costume designer: "In film, sometimes you will be introduced to a character who is on-screen for only thirty seconds or a minute. So the costumer has to find the right prop to distinguish that character quickly without making the person too exaggerated or cartoonlike.

"Jewelry is just a part of the painting that you make, or the odd piece of a puzzle that makes up a character. But you should never see the costume unless it is a story point—you don't want to distract the viewer from the story or the character. Things like pearls really can say a lot. They are the quickest read for a filmgoer. They are classic; they add just a tiny bit a sparkle, a little gloss. Pearls indicate 'I care about my look but I'm understated about it.' People get the message immediately."

Sometimes a character is identified by her pearls. They are part of her persona. Try imagining an actress dressed as Queen Elizabeth I without a pearl. It's impossible. For her role as the queen of pearls, Sarah Bernhardt's pearl-bedecked

*B*oth Bette Davis in 1939 and Salma Hayek in 1999 (opposite, photographed by Matthew Rolston) as the pearl-obsessed Queen Elizabeth I.

costumes were created by Paul Poiret for *Queen Elizabeth* (1912). The recent nostalgia for this ruling Dream Maker helped to nominate costumer Alexandra Byrne for an Academy Award for Cate Blanchett's pearly wardrobe in *Elizabeth* (1998). In the same year, Sandy Powell won an Oscar for the pearl-studded dresses and wigs that Dame Judi Dench wore with great pomp and circumstance in her Academy Award–winning portrayal of the pearl-obsessed Elizabeth in *Shakespeare in Love* (1998). America's own original costumer and fashion designer, Bob Mackie, and Whoopi Goldberg drew applause from nearly 46 million television viewers around the world when the comedienne, dressed as Mackie's version of the Pearl Queen, white face and all, stepped onto the stage in Hollywood to emcee the seventy-first

Academy Awards ceremony, which celebrated the year of Elizabeth on film and the new fashion for regal dressing.

Instead of taking her place onstage for a global commercial broadcast, Ms. Goldberg might have waltzed onto the dance floor of an elaborate costume ball. In her fanciful costume, Goldberg would have fit right in. An ancient social form of creative expression, costume balls are an intimate arena in which to express an alternate persona. England's Queen Elizabeth I adored these events and was known to change her costume two or three times during a single evening. In the court of King James I these evenings were called masques, and in his memoirs the monarch recalls "being not a little delighted with such fluent elegance as made the nights more glorious than the days." Czarist Russia's Empress Elizabeth, known for her propensity for wearing short pants to show off her beautiful legs, ordered transvestite balls, while her successor,

Catherine the Great, enjoyed opening up her balls to the public.

Queen Victoria and her husband, Prince Albert, hosted fancy dress balls. For the Plantagenet Ball in 1842, Victoria dressed as another ruler, Queen Philippa. Her costume included her own infamous diamond bodice ornament, called a stomacher, which was valued at sixty thousand pounds sterling (between four and five million of today's dollars). During Victoria's Silver Jubilee celebration in 1897 England's duchess of Devonshire staged a landmark ball, stating on the invitation that the dress was to be an allegorical or historical costume from before 1815. Couturier Charles Frederick Worth designed the duchess's costume for her portrayal of Zenobia, queen of Palmyra. Topping her dress and bejeweled train, was a gem-encrusted headband and ropes of superb pearls that looped down over her ears and trailed down her dress. Worth also designed an elaborate Louis XV costume for one of her guests, the duke of Marlborough. The expense and

Everyone saw the humor in Bob Mackie's homage to the Virgin Queen designed for Whoopi Goldberg's entrance as emcee of the 1999 Academy Awards ceremony.

Mrs. Arturo López Willshaw's interpretation of a Chinese empress for the spectacular Beistegui Ball in Venice (1951) is encrusted with pearls from the tip of her hairdo to the rim of her fan. OPPOSITE: The Pless family pearls dripped down to the floor, as does this elaborate necklace worn by Daisy, the Princess of Pless, in costume as the Queen of Sheba for the Devonshire House Ball (1897).

extravagance of the duke of Marlborough's velvet costume embroidered with silver, pearls, and diamonds stunned the designer himself. As Worth wrote in his autobiography, "Each pearl and diamond was sewn on by hand, and it took several girls almost a month to complete this embroidery of jewels."

Fifty-four years later Count Charles de Beistegui, heir to an enormous Spanish-Mexican silver fortune, outdid the Devonshires with his famous costumed celebration of his restoration of the eighteenth-century Palazzo Labia in Venice. Beistegui's party, hosted for hundreds of his friends from around the globe on September 3, 1951, has been hailed as the most spectacular ball of the twentieth century. For what was the first major social event after World War II, the eccentric Dream Maker spared no expense. Invitations were distributed six months in advance in order to give guests time to prepare. Like the duchess of Devonshire's ball, Beistegui's affair was de rigueur for the international social set, and guests vied for tickets as fiercely as they competed to make the grandest entrance. American style setter Daisy Fellowes modeled her outfit on a 1750 Tiepolo painting, called *The Americas,* and arrived with a barefooted friend dressed as her parasol-carrying servant. Mrs. Fellowes's dress, combining taffeta with leopard-print chiffon, set a trend for the spotted motif in everything from clothing to luggage to home furnishings.

Instead of negotiating the Venetian canals in the customary gondola, an ornate Chinese junk and weeks of rehearsals helped Mr. and Mrs. Arturo López-Willshaw and their guests make the most spectacular arrival. The Chilean fertilizer tycoon posed as the emperor of China, and his wife, Patricia, wore long fingernail spikes and lots of pearls. Pearls highlighted her towering hairdo, dangled from her ears, encircled her neck, dripped from her clothes, and even outlined her fan.

Since Beistegui's palazzo housed the famed Tiepolo fresco called *The Banquet of Cleopatra,* many women wanted to dress as Cleopatra. Beistegui assigned the role to his friend, the English beauty and eccentric Lady Diana Cooper, and her costume was draped and studded with pearls. Beistegui himself, dressed as the procurator of the Venetian Republic, wore a flowing wig of giant sausage-roll curls and platform shoes that lifted him nearly two feet above his guests.

On November 28, 1966, Truman Capote made a long-held dream come true. For his famous Black and White Ball, held in honor of his friend, *Washington Post* publisher Katherine Graham, the controversial author invited five hundred of his favorite friends—mixing artists, writers, and Hollywood headliners with politicians, entertainers, leading socialites, and a contingent from Garden City, Kansas (the scene of

Capote's groundbreaking book, *In Cold Blood*). As the party drew near, Capote told *WWD*'s Jack Robertson, "It will be the biggest event of the season . . . and the only ball in 25 years that people can attend without having to pay $200 a ticket for charity. It's free. I want people to just come and have fun. . . . But they will have to work. The people will be part of the decoration." Capote's theme called for red decorations and his guests dressed in black and white. "Why use flowers for decoration? . . . People are much more interesting," he concluded.

Some of the guests ordered multiple masks, and a few of the women commissioned as many as three dresses for Capote's night in the Grand Ballroom of New York's Plaza Hotel. Fashion designer Adolfo created over one hundred of the evening's custom-made masks, including those for Merle Oberon and C.Z. Guest. Kenny Lane converted a sparkling necklace, drenched with pearls, into a mask for the daughter of his friend, Italian writer Luigi Barzini. From his perch as designer for Bergdorf Goodman's millinery department, Halston produced many of the sea of feathered and jeweled masks, including a rabbit-eared version in white mink for Candice Bergen. But the young fashion star also hand-painted the most streamlined mask of the night for his friend and future colleague, socialite D. D. Ryan. Halston's black-and-white Kabuki-style mask was a perfect complement to Ryan's walnut-sized white pearl earrings and sleek black hairstyle that was anchored on the crown of her head by a white gardenia.

Even though Capote had one of the last words on the subject, there have been some celebrated balls since his New York City soirée. In 1971, the Guy de Rothschilds hosted the Proust Ball in their home, Château de Ferrières, outside of Paris. "When I walked in, dressed as the Marchesa Casati, no one recognized me. Not even Marie-Hélène [de Rothschild, the hostess]," recalls Marisa Berenson, one of the most exquisite models of the 1970s and 1980s. "I remember it well!" Marisa's disguise, was the creation of costume designer Piero Tosi, known for his wardrobes for Luchino Visconti's films: "Piero said that everybody else at the ball would be wearing typical period dress with corsets and chignons. Casati was a contemporary of Proust's, but she dressed in a more prophetic fashion than others of the time. With her fiery red-dyed hair, white makeup, and black-rimmed eyes; her body-revealing clothes; and a passion for the dramatic, Casati defined an entire era of fashion. She inspired fashion designer Paul Poiret and the great poets, writers, and painters of that period." Costume supplier Umberto Tirelli (also known for his work on Visconti's films and other period pieces) provided the original Poiret gown, the headdress, and other authentic 1920s elements of Berenson's costume. Marisa loved the ropes and ropes of pearls draped down the front of her dress. "A woman in pearls is at her most feminine," she opines. "Pearls are the most adorning ornament for a woman. They make her translucent. You can wear them at any time. I have pink pearls, gray pearls, and white pearls, although my pink and gray ones are fakes. The white ones are big South Sea pearls that my ex-husband got for me in Hong Kong years ago."

Berenson's love of pearls began with early memories of her beloved grandmother, the legendary fashion designer Elsa Schiaparelli. "My grandmother wore pearls all the time," notes Marisa. "She was never without them. I always remember her dressed in black with three strands of big pearls, a big pearl brooch, and her pearl rings. In the evening she wore other incredible jewelry, but during the day she never took these pieces off."

The late Sir Cecil Beaton, who photographed the statuesque Berenson in her Casati costume, was also a guest at the Proust celebration, as he had been at the balls of both Capote and Beistegui. Beaton too enjoyed the idea of stepping out of himself for a few hours, and balls were of special interest to him for both their social and their fantasy value. More than just a fancy party, costume balls have provided a sanctioned outlet for amusement and fantasy.

Photographic historian Gail Buckland, who collaborated with Beaton on two books, remembers Beaton as a wonderful dresser: "The hats and the suits! And he often wore a pearl stickpin. He made fashion fun. He once gave me a lift to Noël Coward's memorial service, and he was dressed entirely in white. I had never seen him quite so radiant. As he put it, 'Noël made it clear that he wanted us to dress as if we were going to a garden party.'

"Cecil was also very intrigued with the way women were able to dress up," Buckland says, explaining the myriad self-portraits of Beaton, including those in women's clothing. Beaton once photographed himself showing off the pearl-embroidered flapper dress that his mother wore for one of his signature mirror portraits. "He coveted the experience that as a male he was denied," Buckland continues. "But as soon as he acknowledged his fascination with fantasy and costume, he indulged his love of dressing up. Sometimes he would change his costume three times at a party because he couldn't decide which character to be."

Beaton's love of theatrical artifice made costume balls defining moments for him. To a natural journalist like Beaton, they were also a matter of important record. From the time he took up his faithful Kodak Brownie camera to photograph socialites and began sending his highly personal fashion and society news

Marisa Berenson, in costume, as the Marchesa Casati in 1971.

to *Vogue* magazine, everything that entered his creative vista was filtered through his discerning taste and underwent his journalistic scrutiny. Many of the important personalities of the twentieth century have passed before his lens, from his friend and mentor, the Honorable Stephen Tennant, to socialite and style maker Lady Diana Cooper, the impeccable duchess of Windsor, Beaton's idol and sometime lover, the enigmatic Greta Garbo—even to pop culture's Andy Warhol and Mick Jagger.

"He knew what he liked, and Cecil was sincere in his love of photography," says Buckland. "He liked beauty, form, and style. He carefully considered the options for lighting, backgrounds, and whether or not he could enlarge on the character of the person. As the photographer for the royal family from 1939 until the 1970s, he wanted to know how he could make them as beautiful as possible.

"Through his eyes, even the queen comes out looking good on the postage stamp," Buckland observes. Some of the most romantic photographs of the Queen Mum, dressed in her Winterhalter-inspired white lace dress and pearls are Beaton's, as are the soft portraits of the pearl-wearing young princesses Elizabeth and Margaret, lounging in the garden with their father.

"Cecil had a very playful side," Buckland continues. "He recognized that we need to have releases in life. Things like fashion are a way of recognizing humanness and gaiety. His contribution was to make people feel good about enjoying life. Beaton understood that these things we call frivolity—even pearls—are really important to us."

Fascinated by mirror images, Cecil Beaton photographed his mother at her dressing table in 1925. Her pearl-beaded evening dress is in the mode of the stylish evening dresses popularized by Coco Chanel—a look Mrs. Beaton accessorized with pearl jewelry.

BELOW: Playing with identity, Beaton, dressed as his mother, poses for society photographer Dorothy Wilding.

*G*race Kelly, Her Serene Highness, the Princess of Monaco; Jacqueline Bouvier Kennedy Onassis; and Lady Diana Spencer, Princess of Wales: collectively, they defined the prevailing image of modern elegance and beauty in the past fifty years and set a standard for the twenty-first century. Each reached the pinnacle of enduring fascination to the public: Grace dominated the entertainment industry, Jackie rose to prominence via the American political scene, and Lady Diana commanded world attention from her royal vantage point at Kensington Palace.

Hollywood was the perfect medium to convey Grace's elegance, poise, and classic American good looks. Grace refined the idea of the girl-next-door, and her aristocratic, pedigreed image propelled her into royal circles. Jackie stepped onto the political platform as the doyenne of Camelot, ushering in an era of cultured modernity and sophistication and becoming the high priestess of grace and elegance. Diana's struggle to balance traditional and new ways to be a princess brought a breath of fresh air into the cloister of British royalty, leaving it a changed institution.

Each of these women broke with their predecessors. They cut their own paths to success and tailored their roles to conform to their personal visions. For example, like Eleanor Roosevelt before her, Jackie was a strong, independent First Lady. However, unlike Mrs. Roosevelt—a tireless humanitarian like her husband—Jackie was unabashedly interested in the arts and historic preservation. Risking criticism for her pursuit of rarefied, sometimes snobbish interests, Jackie persevered. She liked fine furniture, respected classical art, demanded serious music, revered exceptional literature, and spoke three languages. Jackie gave the world a taste of her impeccable style on the day her husband took office as president of the United States, when she donned her Halston pillbox hat with matching beige coat and luxurious sable muff, thereby enthroning herself as the nation's queen and arbiter of style. Jackie used her position to rouse national pride with such projects as restoring the presidential headquarters to its proper status as a federal treasure and museum. She also advocated for the preservation of numerous Washington, D.C., buildings and assisted in the planning of a national cultural center that resulted in the John F. Kennedy Center for the Performing Arts. In essence, Jackie linked the promotion of high-brow culture to the goal of improving the world's perception of American culture. Her success and popularity as America's unofficial ambassador of style is perhaps best illustrated by her husband's comment to a "Vive Jacqui"–cheering Paris crowd at the conclusion of his 1961 state visit: "I am the man who accompanied Jacqueline Kennedy to Paris, and I have enjoyed it."

PAGE 158: *Grace* Kelly in the pearls of her youth and the bracelet that she would wear for many years. RIGHT: **Jackie in Paris, with her signature Kenneth Jay Lane pearls tucked into the neckline of her suit; a timeless gesture that the First Lady turned into a timeless fashion icon.**

A contemporary of Jackie's, Grace Kelly was the first of the three women in this chapter to capture the imagination of the masses. Grace's finely boned features and porcelain complexion helped to launch a career as a model and product spokesperson before she advanced to stage, television, and film acting. A driven performer, Grace pressed for a wider range of Hollywood film roles for women by demanding complex, challenging, and nuanced parts from directors she

admired and befriended, such as Alfred Hitchcock. Movie screens the world over reflected her sleek, luminous beauty and her polished manner, beneath which seemed to smolder passions ready to be stoked. Her performances heralded an era of broader depictions of female roles while reinforcing the traditional image of the blond-haired, blue-eyed Main Line Philadelphia beauty as the American ideal. In her life as a princess, Grace was a curiosity not so much for her beauty; Europeans were already accustomed to beautiful women with titles, even to Americans and middle-class women who had married into their titles. But she was an anomaly in another way. Here was a woman from wealthy but solidly working-class who stepped from the theatrical stage to a royal one with vitality and aplomb. Although Grace's celebrity initially attracted the public, her charm, dignity, and humanity ultimately won her global devotion.

Diana, like Jackie, gained the public's favor around the world in part for her sophistication, which grew increasingly apparent with the years. But Diana's appeal arose, in great measure, from the youthful warmth, verve, and candor that she brought to the House of Windsor. She earned the title "The People's Princess" not only because she literally matured before the public's eyes, but also because she dared to show her humanness: her frailties, compassion, temper, resolve, and genuine concern for pressing global issues. In addition to these qualities—so uncharacteristic of the British royals—she was blessed with dewy good looks, stature, and a trim, athletic figure she proudly worked to maintain. Personality and appearance joined forces to create a princess who disarmed many of her detractors and beguiled the populace.

These three women possessed the physical attributes to make them favored subjects of the camera. Their long, lean bodies showcased fine clothing and turned photographs into compelling works of art. Endowed with high cheekbones, broad shoulders, and swanlike necks, they shared the regal posture and carriage of a person who commands and expects notice. Their ethereal beauty was best seen against a backdrop of chic, understated fashion silhouettes. Though Grace, Jackie, and Diana each developed a unique style, their taste orbited in close proximity to modern versions of traditional garments, updated in luxurious fabrics and accessorized by exquisite but simple jewelry, such as pearls. Grace's use of pearls reflected the discreet, upper-class elegance of the times. Jackie and Diana took more aggressive postures. Jackie treated pearls as a uniform, in the manner of a grown-up schoolgirl. Able to draw from her royal box of showpiece jewelry, Diana took an eclectic route, tasteful but, just as often, sexy. Their

unfettered styles of dress suited their demanding travel and social itin-
eraries, which women around the world began to see as evidence of a
growing place for females at society's helms of influence.

     This self-assured, confident attitude, along with their beauty
and glamour, was integral to the trio's appeal to both men and women.
But certainly their allure was greater than the sum of its parts. In fact, their charisma
may be described as existing *in between* their obviously attractive qualities. The *frisson,*
the energy, generated by the contrast between their wholesome, fresh, well-bred
looks and cool, reserved demeanor made them irresistible. They were at once available and untouchable. They belonged to the people and yet were detached from
them too. Formidable survivors and ingenues at the same time. That they wouldn't
quite fit into neat categories fueled the public's interest as well.

A youthful, Shy Di
chooses appropriately
innocent pearl-and-diamond
earrings for her engagement
portrait by Lord Snowdon.

Grace Kelly, America's fairy-tale princess, was born on November 12, 1929, into a well-heeled Philadelphia family dominated by a striving, self-made patriarch and former Olympic oarsman who had created a small fortune in the bricklaying and construction business. Grace could have done anything she wanted, but to her family's horror, she wanted to be an actress. Taking inspiration from her empathetic supporter, her uncle George Kelly, the well-known playwright, Grace's heart led her to a life of performing. Her acting legacy includes commercials, sixty live television programs in two years, numerous stage performances, and twelve films.

While looking for a newsworthy local angle for their coverage of the Cannes Film Festival in May 1955, the editors of *Paris-Match* magazine arranged a publicity stunt that would change Grace's life forever. The Academy Award–winning American was to meet Prince Rainier III of Monaco, the world's most eligible prince. When Grace's sense of propriety called for a polite thank-you note to the dashing prince after their visit, the letter initiated a correspondence that found them revealing shared experiences, beliefs, and intimacies. This correspondence, perhaps coupled with some earlier counsel from Aristotle Onassis, the Greek shipping magnate, encouraged the monarch to pursue the screen gem from Philadelphia and invite her to become his princess. Onassis, who had business interests in Monaco, had suggested to Rainier that he marry an American movie star; such a union, he said would provide the prince with a companion and an heir, and a star of magnitude could parlay

*G*race Kelly married her prince in 1956, and this photograph by Howell Conant captures the spirit.

her universal presence into a positive impact on Monaco's flagging economy. A private civil ceremony was held in Monaco on April 18, 1956, and the formal church ceremony, with unprecedented press coverage, was celebrated the next day. Grace's friend Hollywood designer Helen Rose created her pearl-edged wedding gown with its veil made from ninety yards of tulle, onto which were sewn hundreds of pearls.

Her performance career served her well for a new role in Monaco, according to her longtime friend Eleanor Lambert, the New York public-relations virtuoso. "She had all the qualities to become royalty very effectively," says Lambert. "She took it on with a natural talent. Dignity. A regal attitude. She was able to detach, to remove herself from the people she was being warm and charming to. That was the regal thing. The Queen Mother is both cozy and cool. Grace had the same ability."

Toward the end of her life, Grace sought an outlet for her pent-up creative energies. She wanted to go back to work, to return to her beloved acting profession, but without the spectacle of a revived Hollywood career. The citizens of Monaco and, for the most part, Rainier vehemently opposed this idea. At the suggestion of one of Grace's friends, a theater producer contacted the princess. Would she be interested in reciting poetry for a benefit fund-raiser? With eagerness and her usual professionalism, she took up the challenge. Grace became known for her moving, expertly delivered poetry readings to raise money for charities. Not long before the car accident that took Grace's life, Princess Diana attended one of Grace's readings at Goldsmith's Hall in London. A caring friendship began when Grace took the opportunity to offer some comfort and advice to a newly engaged and press-besieged Diana. With her characteristic sharp wit and fortitude, Grace commiserated with Diana over the English princess's diminishing privacy but sagely predicted: "It will only get worse!"

From her early days "Grace set a style for the cool blond look," says Lambert, who founded the International Best Dressed Lists, onto which Grace was voted by editors and fashion experts around the world for many years. "She was very cool and collected," continues Lambert. "She didn't strike me as the sort of person who could be told what to wear. Grace was independent." Lambert took Grace shopping for her trousseau, making the rounds of top American designers in New York, including Norman Norell. "Before Grace, people had the perception that blondes were all fussy, gurgly people, with curls and waves like Shirley Temple. Grace, however, had sleek blond hair that she could pull back and look very *Philadelphia Story*. She never looked

*P*earls were her standby, including the double-strand choker that Grace Kelly wore to the Palais de Festivals in Edward Quinn's 1955 photograph.

as though she had a permanent. That must have been very trendsetting then. It's a look that has gone on forever and continues now." Fashion journalist June Weir concurs: "Grace's legacy was her incredible beauty with her magnificent hairstyle that was sleek and classic and perfect. Her face was really her fortune—that and her signature Hermès handbag, twin sweater set, and simple strand of pearls."

We see Grace in pearls in her on-screen life as well as in her private life. In classic 1950s style, Grace wore only pearl jewelry for her role as Lisa Carol Fremont in Alfred Hitchcock's *Rear Window*. In the official engagement photograph of Grace and Prince Rainier, Grace is wearing a two-strand choker similar to the one her mother frequently wore. For her wedding day Grace chose simple pearl-and-diamond earrings to complement her elaborate gown. She inadvertently packed the pearl earrings that she had selected to wear with her going-away suit, so her bridesmaid Judith Balaban Quine, gave Grace the pearl-and-diamond earrings that she had assembled from her own mother's jewelry. As a wedding present, Rainier commissioned a parure of pearls from Van Cleef and Arpels: a three-strand necklace, ear clips, and a triple-strand bracelet of perfectly matched pearls with diamond highlights.

Rita Gam, Grace's friend and roommate from her early Hollywood days, says that Grace wore her jewelry sparingly: "Grace had a lot of jewelry but did not wear it during the day because that was not the kind of lady she was. She would wear one or two strands of pearls during the daytime with a sweater. Anything more elaborate was for formal occasions. I saw her over a number of years, and she always wore pearls in some fashion or another. I never asked her whether or not her pearls were real. I assumed that her parents gave her real pearls as a high school graduation present or for her eighteenth birthday. We joked once about pearls becoming real if you think they are, as in the drama *The Madwoman of Chaillot*, when the character Constance questions the quality of the countess's pearls, saying, 'Suppose I said

*M*other and daughter Caroline both wear pearl bracelets.
OPPOSITE: **Grace goes to the beach with pearls at her wrist.**
Howell Conant, her personal photographer, documents it all.

your pearls were false!' The countess admits that her pearls were once fake, but claims they became real, which confuses and irritates Constance. The countess then explains: 'Everyone knows that little by little, as one wears pearls, they become real.'

"Grace was particularly lucky in that her skin tone was exquisite with pearls. Knowing the look she wanted, Grace always utilized pearls. Wearing pearls was also a part of that period. In that era pearls portrayed a woman's position in life. People bought pearls to upgrade their look. Pearls were synonymous with wealth and proper ladies and royals. Grace was a product of her era as well as the result of her own individual style. But it's not just about her look. Her legacy continues because Grace had depth and quality. She continues to represent elegance of look, personality, and soul."

Jacqueline Bouvier grew up in the cultivated world of horses, custom-made clothing, and Miss Porter's School for Girls in Farmington, Connecticut. After making her debut in 1947, Jackie was expected, and directed, to marry well and raise a family in the upper echelons of society. She was a bright, inquisitive self-starter, unfit for a life without challenge and adventure. Jackie had her own agenda for entering the world of influence and power, which started with a job as a roving reporter for *The Washington Times-Herald*. This post led her to ask friends for an introduction to the rising young senator from Massachusetts, whom she wanted to profile. Her resulting meeting with John F. Kennedy sparked a quiet courtship that culminated in the union of what would become our nation's youngest and most stylish president and First Lady. When viewed with the benefit of hindsight, Jackie's contributions were many, but perhaps her earliest legacy was the way she dressed. *WWD,* the fashion trade publication that followed her every move and became the Jackie-watchers' bible, dubbed Jackie "Her Elegance." With Jackie, "fashion entered politics," John Fairchild observed in *The Fashionable Savages,* written during his tenure as publisher of *WWD* and founder of *W* magazine. "Mrs. Kennedy defied tradition by being chic. For the first time America had a First Lady setting the Taste of the Land." Her main criteria for attire—embodied in simple, modern designs well-constructed in quality materials—led Jackie to the best European and American designers, such as Balenciaga, Givenchy, Dior, and, later, to Chanel and Valentino. Jackie is said to have spent twenty to thirty thousand dollars on clothes while her husband was campaigning (the number differs depending on whether you read accounts by *New York Times* society reporter Charlotte Curtis or the original report in *WWD*, which stated that Jackie and her mother-in-law *together* had spent that amount). When the size of her clothing budget and the continental origins of her wardrobe came under attack, Jackie asked Oleg Cassini to become her official couturier, which brought a well-connected American designer to the service of a discriminating and educated client.

In partnership with Cassini, Jackie dictated the pared-down look that seemed to echo America's forward-looking orientation and sixties optimism. Clothing manufacturers worldwide copied her sleeveless skimmer dresses, suits with short boxy jackets, low-heeled pumps, pillbox hats and berets, long leather gloves, oversized sunglasses, and chain-handled handbags for daytime. During Jackie's brief tenure in the White House, American clothing styles saw the first hints of their budding importance to and influence on world fashion.

Jackie Kennedy at the wedding breakfast for 1,200 guests at Hammersmith Farm, in Newport, on September 12, 1953.

Throughout her lifetime Jackie consistently reached for her pearls when in the public eye. From the White House she started a much-emulated trend of tucking pearl necklaces into the necklines of the round-necked dresses and suits that she frequently wore by day and the signature body-skimming gowns she wore at night. Even after her marriage to Aristotle Onassis—from whom she received an estimated $5 million worth of jewelry in the first year of their union—she continued to appear in public most frequently in pearls. And later, in her private life as a working woman in New York City, she could often be spotted in a single-strand graduated choker, a twisted seed-pearl necklace, or a single strand of oversized baroque pearls.

Countless photographs of Jackie's life bear witness to her reliance on pearls: at her wedding; on the presidential campaign trail; with Jack and baby Caroline; with young John, who is shown pulling on his mother's triple-strand necklace; in Paris; in India; in Nantucket; at the opera; even on a stroll in Central Park. "Whenever Jackie wore pearls, whether she wore them with a daytime dress or a strapless evening gown, they were always appropriate," June Weir observes. Grace Mirabella adds, "When Jackie entered the room, *she* was the focus of attention, not her clothing. That's where pearls fit in: they work very perfectly with almost every element of clothing that is otherwise handsome and beautiful."

Often people are surprised to learn that many of Jackie's pearls were imitations. "One of the most famous pearls we've sold recently are Jackie's, and they were fake," says Sotheby's jewelry expert, John Block. The auction house garnered $200,000 for the original three-strand necklace, which Jackie had bought from New York's Kenneth Jay Lane, for less than $200. The Philadelphia-based collectibles company, the Franklin Mint, purchased this KJL necklace during Sotheby's auction of Jackie's personal effects in 1996. Costume jewelry specialist Carolee Friedlander bought a sixty-inch rope of faux pearls and a pair of leaf-shaped crystal pavé earrings hung with drop pearls at the auction. That September, her company, Carolee, launched a seventeen-item collection of pearl jewelry inspired by Jackie, at Bloomingdale's, Saks Fifth Avenue, and Neiman Marcus. "The collection is an ongoing effort for us," says Carolee. "We feel like Jackie is living forever. She is timeless."

In true youngster form, John F. Kennedy, Jr., pulls at his mother's pearls (1960).

Jackie retained her basic style throughout her life but made subtle changes to her wardrobe to suit a professional and more private personal life after the death of Onassis. She began a career as a book editor in 1975, working first for Viking and later for Doubleday. At the office, with her bouffant hairstyle and outsized sunglasses, she cut a chic figure in a pair of slim trousers and an elegant sweater. Continuing to follow her preservation ideals, Jackie lent her auspicious name to numerous charitable efforts, most notably the campaigns for New York's Central Park Conservancy and Municipal Art Society. Each of these endeavors was graced with her hallmarks—quality and elegance.

Outside of her roles as First Lady, wife, working mother, and tastemaker, Jackie was quite outspoken about her commitment to her home and children and is famous for her insistence that nothing in life is more important than raising your children well. At her funeral her son, the late John F. Kennedy, Jr., summarized his mother very clearly when he spoke of her "love of words, the bonds of home and family, and her spirit of adventure."

Jackie and sister, Lee, in India. OPPOSITE: Slim Aaron's portrait of Jackie at the April in Paris Ball in New York in 1955, dressed in one of her signature white gowns and pearls.

With a nod from the Queen Mother, England's thirty-two-year-old bachelor Prince Charles plucked the chaste Lady Diana Spencer out of the flock as his proper mate. Diana had the right lineage, one dating back to Saxon times and including the first Sir Winston Churchill, among other royal connections. Almost immediately, Diana introduced a more contemporary way of living into Kensington Palace. Her sensibilities and approach to life—far more genial and relaxed than Prince Charles's stiffer brand—were soon a source of obvious and public vexation for the royal family. An ingenuous nineteen-year-old bride, Diana unapologetically labored to pull her reluctant groom out of architectural preservation meetings and into London nightlife, and at the same time struggled to shelter her domestic life from the disapproving scrutiny of the Windsors. The willful Diana, known as "Duchess" to her family, "seemed so composed, so very sure of herself," Robert Lacey writes in his book *Princess*. "She knew what she wanted, and she was good at getting it." She was not, however, completely prepared for the onslaught of public attention and the vigilance it demanded. For example, Diana slipped into a strapless black gown for the couple's first public appearance at a Goldsmith's Hall benefit. Her breast nearly slipped out of her stylish dress as she and Charles alighted from their car to greet the crowd, and the repercussions set her back a step or two. Diana made other missteps too. She wore clothes that were too sheer, too dowdy, too fussy, too accessorized; she

Standing hat and shoulders above the crowd at the Royal Ascot horse races in June 1989, Diana accessorizes her pink suit with the three-strand choker given to her by her parents when she was eighteen years old.

confided in the press inappropriately; she revealed her eating disorder; she took lovers. But most Britons responded to her frailty, and the rest of the world followed, touched by her determination, her humanity, her burgeoning movie-star glamour. However flawed, and using Jackie Onassis as her model, Diana did it her way. She treated her children with compassion and insisted that they experience, within the confines of a rareified existence, life's everyday joys and hardships. Diana developed her own list of charitable beneficiaries, from AIDS organizations to groups that sought the elimination

The Prince and Princess of Wales with William and Harry in Venice in 1985.

of land mines worldwide. She asked for a precedent-setting divorce with a firm set of terms. Diana never stopped testing and pushing the parameters—until a self-assured mature princess, who dared to fall in love with a man outside the traditional aristocratic circle, emerged in control of herself and a destiny that was cut short by alcohol and recklessness. In the end the royal family, which had tightened its ranks against her, capitulated to Diana's charisma in the public's eyes. She won the right to keep the title of princess and, in death, was given a dignified funeral by the begrudging Windsors.

The tallest of the three mythmakers, Diana stood nearly six feet three inches in high-heeled shoes. Schoolchildren still talk about how she always knelt down to their level to converse with them; adults refer to her regal carriage but point out that her height never intimidated them. As one American admirer, June Weir, describes Diana's stately presence: "She always made you feel that she was proud to be tall. You almost wished you were six feet yourself. And she did have the grace of a dancer, which is what she always wanted to be."

"Diana's appeal as a postmodern icon resides solely in her ability to renew and transform herself—and by racing just slightly ahead of our imagination, to hold us in constant thrall," contends Cathy Horyn in a cover article for *Vanity Fair* magazine. For the feature, Diana modeled for photographer Mario Testino her favorite styles from an upcoming auction of dresses she had worn during her life as the wife of the Prince of Wales. It was Prince William's idea that Diana auction the clothes, to both rid herself of the past after her royal divorce and raise money for one of her favorite causes: the search for a cure for AIDS.

Diana renewed herself several times. Royal watcher Judy Wade outlines Diana's transitions for *Vanity Fair*: "First it was demure Di, then disco Di, then *Dynasty* Di; now it's dedicated Di." Diana expressed her stages of growing up through her clothes. She learned to speak with clothes, and used the language with the skill of a seasoned orator. During her youthful beginnings, there were the cumbersome fashions from every designer in London, which society-page editors scurried to identify. Still unsure, she tried racier outfits, and shocked some onlookers with her public display of spandex gym clothes.

Dynasty Di wore modern but somewhat exaggerated clothes with a dash of the glitz that Nolan Miller gave actress Joan Collins for her lavish wardrobe for the television series *Dynasty*. From pearl-studded gowns, such as the one dubbed the "Elvis Dress," with its all-over pearl jacket and stand-up collar, to the famous off-the-shoulder velvet evening gown by Victor Edelstein that she wore on her visit to the White House (where she took to the dance floor with John Travolta), Diana telegraphed her developing sexual allure and independence, foreshadowing her eventual media showdown with Charles. Her use of fashion as a first line of defense in the public battle she waged with Charles is best illustrated by her spectacular appearance in the sexy black chiffon by London designer Christina Stambolian, which the press called her "Vengeance Dress." She wore it the night that Charles confessed on television his continuing affair with Camilla Parker-Bowles. Diana upstaged Charles by showing up for a dinner at the

Serpentine Gallery in Hyde Park wearing this short, clingy black chiffon dress with its flowing panel; bright red nails, freshly shorn hair, and her signature seven-row pearl choker with a giant, oval sapphire-and-diamond clasp completed the look. The striking photographs of a stunning and assertive Diana bumped Charles from the front pages of newspapers the world over. Clearly, the world's sympathies and attention were with its princess.

Whether young, innocent, and overdecorated—or dressed to kill in the minimal chic she adopted during the last few years of her life—Diana always wore jewels. Discreet gold loops graced her ears when she went out into the fields of Angola to help search for land mines. She honored King Fahd of Saudi Arabia in 1986 by wearing a pair of pendant earrings in the shape of his nation's signature, the crescent moon; the diamond drops were glittery fakes from London's Butler and Wilson.

Pearls were her favorite gems, and she had lots. Her parents gave her a single strand of pearls with a sapphire clasp that she wore throughout her life. She also favored a longer strand with a sapphire clasp that had been a wedding present. Prince Charles bought her a striking necklace from Leo de Vroomen, and Diana had its large dark gray and natural pearls reworked into other jewels. Another of her favorite looks was to don two twisted rows of pearls with a pearl cluster clasp. When Diana was married, she wore the Spencer family tiara that both of her sisters had worn, and she borrowed her mother's pearl-and-diamond earrings. Diana's wedding gown was highlighted with mother-of-pearl sequins and pearl-embroidered lace. When Diana and Charles left their wedding reception in a horse-drawn carriage, the princess was wearing the five-strand pearl choker with a large pearl-and-diamond clasp and a pearl-drop pendant that her sister had worn to the nuptials.

Her wedding present from the Queen Mother was a large oval sapphire surrounded by two rows of diamonds, similar to the queen's Prince Albert brooch. Diana later mounted the sapphire as the centerpiece of her aforementioned signature seven-row pearl necklace. From Queen Elizabeth, Diana received the lover's knot tiara with its nineteen perfect pearl drops, copied for Queen Mary by Garrard in 1914. From the emir of Qatar, the royal couple received a set of pearl jewelry including a watch, rings, cuff links, and earrings. The prince of Jordan presented a multicolored stone-and-gold choker with pearl fringe.

The pearl choker became Diana's trademark; she wore chokers on all occasions. Just as she started a fashion for short, backswept hairstyles, Diana revived the trend for this multistrand necklace. Queen Mary had worn them, as had Queen

Alexandra before her. Diana's first choker—three rows of pearls, with a turquoise-and-pearl cluster clasp—was a gift from her family when she was eighteen years old. She wore it turned to the front or back, depending upon the color of her clothes. Diana eventually changed the clasp to an all-pearl version. She wore other chokers, including one borrowed from Queen Elizabeth—four rows of pearls with a large oval diamond-studded centerpiece. Diana had no compunction about wearing imitations, either: her two-row choker with a small sapphire-and-diamond clasp is a blatant fake from New York's Kenneth Jay Lane. The duchess of Kent liked it so much that she bought the identical necklace. Also faux were the pearls Diana knotted down the back of a low-cut velvet dress—the same ones upon which she sported a nineteenth-century diamond-and-amethyst cross when she attended a 1987 fund-raising gala dinner at Garrard, the crown jewellers, dressed as Queen Elizabeth I. Like most modern women, Diana owned wonderful costume copies of classic styles, like her pearl earrings set in circles of rhinestones.

There are, and always have been, other women who are stylish or accomplished, or both. But the three women we present here were different. Women wanted to be like them and men wanted to have them. They did things their way and invited people to come along. They took criticism but were well armed with a steely reserve. They were the Untouchables and the world applauded their status. Jackie had the chicest style, Grace had the icy cool, and Lady Diana had raciness and great charm. They helped create the image, and we held them up as universal style gurus. Time will tell if they maintain their places on these pedestals. The list of untouchable glamour girls is waiting to grow.

Diana set the trend, but she and her sister Sarah both enjoyed wearing their own versions of pearl collars. Princess Diana's slip dress by John Galliano for Christian Dior is a clear example of the sleek, sophisticated style she was developing. Her signature pearl-and-sapphire choker is part of a collection estimated to be worth more than $27 million at the time of her death (August 31, 1997). Four days after her sister's fatal automobile accident in Paris, Lady Sarah McCorquodale, six years older than Diana, was placed in charge of the Diana, Princess of Wales Memorial Fund and has served as one of the fund's three founding trustees.

W

hen worn throughout a lifetime, pearls develop a rich patina—a deeper luminescence that reflects the warmth of their wearer. Their soft, natural glow is an eternal light.

The women on these final pages were selected because they represent all of the human qualities that are valued in pearls. Pearls are compelling in their natural beauty. They have depth and character that improve with time. Pearls require special care and nurturing to mature and develop properly. They exist outside the whims of fashion. And they have everlasting style.

Nowhere are these thoughts and the long-term benefits of wearing pearls more

LIGHTS

PAGE 184: C.Z. Guest recently added South Sea pearls to her collection; here, her eternal mix of stalwart pride and grace as seen through the lens of Bruce Weber.

ABOVE: C.Z. Guest and socialite Chris Dunphy enjoy a light moment at the Polo Ball in Palm Beach (1954).

OPPOSITE: Sharing much in common, including pearls as their signature jewel, C.Z. Guest and *grande dame* Mrs. Jacques Balsan, the former Consuelo Vanderbilt and duchess of Marlborough, are captured chatting in Palm Beach. C.Z.'s natural pearl necklace is from her mother. Instead of her renowned nineteen-strand pearl collar with diamond dividers, Mrs. Balsan chose four strands of natural white pearls and attached gemstone clips at the sides of the deep-square neckline of her dress for the evening.

apparent than in recent photographic portraits of America's own C.Z. Guest and Brooke Astor. The vision of Mrs. Guest, in her late seventies, reinforces the eternal appropriateness of this celebrated traditionalist and her iridescent gems. She is still a swan, as author Truman Capote called her in the 1950s: "For a swan is invariably the result of adherence to some aesthetic system of thought, a code transposed into a self-portrait; what we see is the imaginary portrait precisely projected." In other words, C.Z. has remained true to herself. And true to her pearls.

The sight of a radiant, slightly impish Mrs. Astor, at ninety-six years old, with her wide-brimmed hat and three-strand pearl necklace reveals with great clarity the integral relationship between people and their pearls. Mrs. Astor always wears pearls. Call it breeding, call it an expression of security and the traditional status attached to these opalescent gems. Brooke Astor stands as a symbolic illustration for the conjecture that when a woman wears pearls, it is she, not her jewels, who shines.

Mrs. Astor may not know why, but she acknowledges her attachment to the mystical gem. "I never go out without pearls on," says the woman whose *joie de vivre* runs from the tip of her toes to the twinkle in her eye. "I couldn't possibly live without pearls. I don't know what it is. I've grown up with them. They have been so much a part of my life—always.

"My family was not particularly well off," she continues, "but my grandmother said that every lady wears pearls. And so I started wearing pearls at about age seven or eight. I had a little string around my neck, and my mother and grandmother started to put pearls on it. They were tiny pearls, and they weren't worth much, but the necklace grew. I didn't wear them in the daytime, and I didn't wear them in school, but I did wear them in the afternoon."

During a trio of marriages, the most devoted of which was her union with W. Vincent Astor, Brooke acquired what she describes as "nice" pearl necklaces. "Of course, I have daytime pearls and I have evening pearls," she chortles. "I have three strings which I wear every day; in the morning and the afternoon, and sometimes in the evening. My evening pearls are bigger and they have diamonds around helping them to be strong. Sometimes the pearls are hanging from the diamonds—or the diamonds are hanging from them," she muses about her bib necklace from Verdura jewelers. When worn, the gems seem to float against her skin. "I have not bought any pearls in years. Mine are old but they are real pearls," she divulges, then adds with sprightly abandon: "I have some fake pearls that I wear out in the country—in the evening with a tea gown."

Some of the portraits on these pages were taken when their subjects were new to their celebrated trails through life. But the fascinating aspect of the images is that the women exude the same sense of strength and character in their youth that they have come to represent as members of an exclusive roster of arbiters of style. Babe Paley was married to her first husband, Stanley G. Mortimer, Jr., and working as a fashion editor for *Vogue* when the magazine asked her to pose for what would become a hallmark photograph in the oeuvre of Horst P. Horst (1946).

Barbara Cushing Mortimer Paley reached for perfection—in her looks, her surroundings, a second marriage that was governed by wealth and power, and a coterie of friends drawn from the highest ranks of the business, intellectual, and social elites. John Fairchild and his editors referred to Mrs. Paley as a goddess and dubbed her "the Ultimate." In *The Fashionable Savages* Fairchild writes: "Babe Paley gives the impression she doesn't care about fashion. She always looks right. She looks better than right." And she dressed for herself, not someone else. Fairchild praises her aristocratic look and gracious nature: "She couldn't be more unpretentious, she couldn't be more natural and more interested in you, the person she is talking to."

However, her strong hold over the art of perfection might have cost Mrs. Paley her life: she smoked two packages of cigarettes a day to control both her weight and the stress of an ever-demanding husband. Even in death, Babe was gracious and

Mrs. Stanley G. Mortimer, Jr. (who would later marry CBS's Bill Paley), took time out from her job as an editor at *Vogue* magazine to pose for Horst. To the Traina-Norell jersey dress, Babe added her own pearl necklace and, as the March 1, 1946, issue says, "a wonderful scramble of bracelets."

exacting to the point of planning every last detail of her own funeral, including an allowance for seasonal menus.

Babe loved jewels, and she could be counted on for her ethereal pearls. She often wore a necklace of multiple rows of tiny pearls through which she threaded a scarf. Other times, she doubled and twisted the rope so that it seemed as though a ruffle of baby's breath encircled her neck. A black-and-white pearl ring was part of her daytime arsenal. Another long pearl necklace was twisted into a three-strand choker to become the footlight of her long swan's neck in the consummate Horst photograph of Babe. Wearing a blue-and-black skimmer, Babe is shown with her ubiquitous cigarette in hand, and her wrist is covered with bracelets—gold links in combination with pearls and pearl necklaces twisted and stacked for their glamorous effect. The picture is a classic illustration of the everlasting quality that Babe brought to her style. Even though clothing, hairstyles, and accessories are more relaxed today, her style remains as fresh and commanding as it was in her day. She had the confidence of her appeal.

Babe was so confident of her fashion sense that she was able to personalize the signature of the designer who invented relaxed modern styling. To suit her own taste, Babe slipped a long scarf around the neck of her classic Chanel braid-trimmed suit. John Fairchild was highly impressed: "She is the only woman I have seen who can wear a Chanel and make Chanel's Chanel a Paley style." To the man who some thought was both judge and jury in the fashion arena, Babe had turned the trim, tailored look into something "more feminine."

The star of *A Girl in Every Port* (1928) and other films of the twenties, Louise Brooks includes among her legacies her leading role in one of the all-time classic portraits of pearls. The stark simplicity of this black-and-white photograph, the clean lines of both her little black dress and cropped hair, and the purity of the long rope of pearls are as elegant as they timeless.

The images of these tastemakers are so revealing and so powerful that even if we knew nothing about how each of them grew and matured, it would take very little effort to imagine the richness of the evolving relationship between these women and pearls. The images themselves have ripened and are possibly more evocative today than they were yesterday. The pictures, like their subjects, are everlasting. For example, the graphic 1920s profile of actress Louise Brooks is a dramatic reminder of the long-term strength, dignity, and unadulterated beauty of pearls.

By studying some of the visual portraits and verbal sketches of those who have worn pearls throughout history, we can learn a lot about people and style, and discern something about the nature of jewelry as it relates to its wearer. In this chapter we are also paying tribute to those rare individuals who have not only understood style but moved beyond it. Their glow is eternal.

Why are all of these women such Eternal Lights? Some of them have created fashion, and some have become the fashion. But none have ignored it altogether. While they observe and absorb the waves of trends, these self-styled leaders have filtered these changes into their unique vision of themselves. Their long association with pearls reflects the rich variations on a magnificent pearl.

The ingredients that go into the creation of everlasting style are much like the layers of a pearl. When you combine the individual layers, you create a lasting gem. In order to create their own styles, these women start with a layer of indifference to the opinions of others. It isn't enough to have the right dress or the right suit one season. Style steps into the certainty that the way you look best is the way you will dress. The ultimate tastemakers of this century—Coco Chanel, Jackie Kennedy Onassis, C.Z. Guest, Babe Paley, the adventuresome Elsie de Wolfe, the elusive Louise Brooks—took the time to study themselves from the inside out. Through a long, hard look in the mirror and some judicious experimentation, they assessed their figures and knew which colors, silhouettes, and fabrics look best. They defined a hairstyle and sifted through a host of cosmetic options until they found possibly two that were suitable. Then these women stuck to their self-styled choices. They could add or subtract an element, but the established parameters acted as their guides.

The portrait for *Vogue* honoring Jacqueline Bouvier as the winner of the magazine's prestigious Prix de Paris contest (1951). Jackie places a pin at the neckline of her dress to complement her double-strand pearl choker.

Dauntless tastemakers are not only arbiters of fashion; they are proficient in all the social arts. Entertaining becomes an art form for women of style, even if it is accomplished on a very private scale. For example, Elsie de Wolfe, the fearless decorator who practically invented the field, popularized the cocktail party and even created her own elixir, called a Pink Lady; equal parts gin, grapefruit juice, and Cointreau. Elsie also invented things like parquet flooring and created the passion for chintz. But throughout her various lives as actress, hostess extraordinaire, and inventive decorator, Elsie had her conventional side. Just as she eventually married and took her title as Lady Mendl, she relied on the tried-and-true wisdom of pearls. "The first thing Elsie did when she earned ten dollars was to buy a string of pearls," Tony Duquette remarked about his mentor, just before his death in 1999. "She just had to have them, and she was never without them."

Elsie, like all leaders, knew where to apply her energies. She was comfortable as a career woman, creative adviser, and author of magazine columns and books offering household tips and advice on decorating. Elsie had studied her face and figure since childhood, in an effort to find a style that would minimize what she considered unattractive features and play up her slim shape and ebullient personality. This meant she was at ease with her appearance. The best testimony to her self-knowledge is a wonderfully eccentric photograph of Elsie sitting in bed under a feathered throw, surrounded by her favorite flowers and a wedge-shaped reading pillow, which was also her invention. Amidst all this quirkiness—notice the bow-tied netting encircling her head—Elsie is wearing her three-strand necklace of graduated pearls. Pearls were her anchor.

The Eternal Lights are aware of their responsibilities in life and religiously fulfill them. Mrs. Astor was known for putting her idea of friendship and a personal life aside to devote herself to the care of Vincent Astor, her complicated second husband. Upon his death, Brooke was placed in charge of his foundation, and she took her charge seriously: to give it all away before she died. By investing judiciously, the Medal of Freedom–winning philanthropist has overseen the distribution of $175 million to world-renowned cultural institutions such as the New York Public Library and to initiatives such as the creation of outdoor living spaces in public housing. She

With her quirks wonderfully in evidence and her pearls in their place, this late photograph of the pioneering actress, decorator, and hostess Elsie de Wolfe illustrates the eternal style, creativity, and self-assurance of one of America's unique individuals.

explained to *The New Yorker*'s Brendan Gill, in an article published in 1997, when she was ninety-five years old, that her own personal fortune was to be divided among the "crown jewels of New York City": the Metropolitan Museum of Art, the New York Public Library, the Pierpont Morgan Library, the Wildlife Conservation Society, and Rockefeller University.

The elements of style could perhaps be condensed to a lesson in "selfs"—self-knowledge, self-determination, self-awareness, self-presentation, and self-expression. But the pivotal ingredients, understood by the Eternal Lights, are, finally, the ability to step out of the self and to honor others. And to face life with an almost innocent sense of adventure and glee. Mrs. Guest is contagious in her zest for living. And Mrs. Astor radiates an irresistible sense of joy and curiosity about life. Whether she is walking anonymously through Bergdorf Goodman on a rainy, bleak winter afternoon to keep herself up-to-date on fashion and style, or attending the celebration for the renovation of New York's historic Grand Central Station, or writing about manners for *Vanity Fair* magazine, Mrs. Astor is a guiding light. She is the beacon who burnishes pearls so that they can be passed on to the next generation. Ultimately, like their wearers, pearls are fragile and ephemeral. But the luster of the relationship between people and pearls fills our thoughts and our sentiments as the circle of pearls continues. May the luminescence of Mrs. Astor and her fellow Eternal Lights shine forever.

Even at ninety-seven, with her ubiquitous pearls in full view, Brooke Astor retains a twinkle in her eye and the boundless vitality that propels an eternal spirit.

PEARLS OF WISDOM

A GUIDE TO BUYING AND OWNING PEARLS

The Art of Buying a Pearl

When you want to buy pearl jewelry, what do you look for? What are the qualities that make one pearl stand out over another? First, decide whether you are looking for natural, cultured, or imitation pearls. Most of the women in this book have owned or enjoyed at least two of these categories, if not the full range. Choosing which variety is right for you is a matter of personal opinion, taste, and budget. Plenty of fake pearls have waltzed the night away at stately occasions, while natural pearls have traveled the world. That's one of the marvelous things about pearls: they belong everywhere, and often only their wearer knows whether they're worth a fortune or a pittance.

A contemporary choker from the Chanel Fine Jewelry collection of 18k gold, diamonds, cultured pearls, and a central South Sea pearl.

If you have decided upon natural or cultured pearls, there are five general criteria for evaluating the quality and the value of a pearl. These standards pertain to the gem's color, luster, shape, size, and surface. The Cultured Pearl Associations of America and Japan and *Modern Jeweler Magazine* have prepared a chart (see page 208) that illustrates these characteristics in a simple, graphic fashion.

Finally, you will want to select the right place to buy pearls, whether that is a jeweler, department or specialty store, or even an auction house. Let's begin by addressing the question of choosing a pearl variety.

Do you want natural, cultured, or imitation pearls?

The following is a quick summary of the different types of pearls. A natural pearl is a spontaneous response to a naturally occurring irritant, such as a bit of shell or a parasite. Natural pearls have no artificially inseminated core or nucleus around which the mollusk makes the pearl by building layer upon layer of iridescent nacre. Natural pearls should come with laboratory certification documenting their authenticity and indicating their quality, as there is no official rating system. The words "natural pearls" should be stated on your proof of purchase. Reputable auction houses, for example, always include the laboratory report with the descriptions of fine pearls.

A nucleus, such as a piece of shell from another oyster, or a round bead, is placed surgically inside the oyster or mussel to stimulate the production of a cultured pearl. The thickness of the nacre is the key element in determining the quality of a cultured pearl. Most fine jewelers know the difference between a very thin coating and one with a healthy thickness. A Japanese cultured Akoya pearl with a nacre thickness of 0.5 mm or more is a very fine specimen, while 0.25 mm is very thin and the minimum for any lasting value. With a magnifying loupe, check for cracks, dents, and breaks in the nacre; and under a bright light, inspect the drill hole for signs of quality and of thickness. If the luster is rich and clearly reflects nearby objects, the nacre is likely to be of top quality. A rainbow or colorful orient dancing across the surface of a pearl is indicative of thick, healthy nacre. The jeweler should provide this information or allow you to have the pearl tested at a laboratory.

Imitation pearls, also known as "faux," "fake," "simulated," or even "semi-cultured," are made from glass, plastic, or mother-of-pearl beads that have been dipped in a mixture of ground fish scales and lacquer (known as "pearl essence" or "essence d'orient") or in a similar plastic coating. (On the descending scale of value, some imitations are painted to look like pearls, and others are simply dyed plastic rounds.) Luster, again, is a good indicator of quality. Good fakes are made of glass beads that have been dipped in an iridescent paste enough times to fool the eye into thinking the pearl is real. The cheaper varieties are usually of lighter weight because they are made from hollow-core plastic beads, and the coating is lackluster. And cheaper varieties are often coated to produce a very shiny surface. Shine is the inexpensive substitute for luster.

Here are a few quick tests to distinguish the various types of pearls: Natural pearls are rarely uniform and will feel gritty when rubbed against your tooth, although the only way to verify that a pearl is truly natural is with an X ray. Use the loupe to examine the drill hole. The smaller the hole, the greater the chance that the pearl is a natural one, since pearls are sold by weight, and a smaller hole would maintain the greatest weight. Also look for brown spotting or a dark line between the nucleus and the conchiolin, and for surface shadows (usually parallel lines) from the nucleus which show through fakes and cultured pearls with very thin nacre. Higher quality cultured pearls have thicker layers of nacre that obliterate dark shadows.

What are the five universal criteria for determining the quality of a pearl?

Just as you evaluate the four Cs (color, clarity, cut, and carat) in a faceted diamond,. when buying pearl jewelry, be alert to the gem's color, luster, shape, size, and surface, characteristics that determine its quality and affect its beauty and value. Of these five traits, luster is the most important. Rich luminosity is not only beautiful, it is usually indicative of first-rate quality, and superior luster can also camouflage slight imperfections on the surface. Here is a brief description of each of the defining characteristics:

COLOR   The color of a pearl is obtained through several sources, including the mollusk itself, the water in the region, the pearl's nucleus, the conchiolin (nature's glue which bonds the layers of the pearl together), even specific cells within the aragonite layers. Black-lipped oysters produce both black and white pearls, while white-lipped varieties are limited to white only. Most naturally black pearls come from the South Pacific (Tahiti and other French Polynesian islands, and the Cook Islands), and a few are still found on the coast of California's Baja peninsula. Gold or yellow pearls are found in Sri Lanka and Myanmar (formerly Burma). Greenish pearls come from Australia, and the wonderfully creamy white pearls hail from the Persian Gulf and the Red Sea. If a pearl retains its natural color, it should be verified on the sales receipt or the laboratory report. Most white cultured pearls today are bleached to make the white color more uniform. Americans like their pearls with a pink hue, while Europeans prefer cream or white. Middle Easterners usually opt for the cream or gold shades, as do South Americans. The final selection of color depends on personal preference, but you should always check your color choice against your skin tone. Black pearls have been in and out of vogue ever since Empress Eugénie introduced and popularized them in the nineteeth century. Ranging from light to very dark gray, with silver, green, or aubergine overtones, these black pearls figure prominently in the recent fascination with colored pearls. Also popular today are pink, lavender, blue, orange, and gold pearls.

LUSTER   Luster is the characteristic that distinguishes pearls from all other gems. Look at a good-quality, healthy pearl and take note of the glow that seems to emanate from within as it complements the colorful rainbowlike shimmer on the surface. Good luster is actually the result of the refraction and reflection of light through the layered, crystalline structure of the nacre. In its booklet *How to Buy a Pearl* (available at the pearl counter), Tiffany & Co. offers a helpful tip for determining the quality of luster: "To check luster, stand with the light to your back. The sharper the reflection of light in the pearl, the higher the luster." Other experts prefer a more romantic standard: the clearer the reflection of your face in the surface of a pearl, the higher the quality. A beautiful pearl must have a bright surface, a deep-seated glow, and the ability to clearly mirror objects within its vision. A pearl that is dull, chalky, or only superficially brilliant is not acceptable as a gem-quality pearl.

SHAPE   Today, the most popular pearl shape is perfect roundness, thanks in part to the quantity of round pearls made available with the advent of cultured pearls and controlled pearl farming. Nearly round (three-quarter- or off-round) pearls are often used as less expensive alternatives to rounds. Historically, oval, teardrop, and pear-shaped pearls were treasured for their myriad uses—as hair decorations, drop earrings, and ornaments on an array of jewelry and clothing, from the simplest brooch or necklace to the most elaborate embroidered gown. Irregular baroque shapes are favored for the rich play of light reflected from their uneven surfaces.

SIZE Pearl diameters are measured in millimeters, and the price increases incrementally with every half-millimeter increase in size. Japanese cultured Akoya pearls range in size from 2 mm to 10 mm. South Sea pearls start at 8 mm and can reach the colossal jawbreaker size of the 23 mm pearl, cultured by Australia's premier pearl farmer, Nicholas Paspaley, in 1999. Pearls in the most popular necklaces average 7mm, which is about the same size as a 1-carat diamond. Seventy percent of all gem-quality pearls are used for necklaces, the 16- to 18-inch single strand being the most popular. The average price for a 16- to 18-inch choker of medium to better quality round Japanese Akoya pearls ranging in size from 6.5 mm to 7 mm is $1,500. Unless the pearls are perfectly matched in size (which is rare and much more costly), in a uniform strand of pearls a variance of 0.5 mm in diameter among the pearls is common and acceptable. In a graduated strand pearl size is quoted from the largest gem (usually placed front and center) to the smallest. The average size of the rest of the pearls should also be stated and included on your receipt.

SURFACE The richer the luster and more opalescent the surface, the more desirable the pearl. The prized pearl is of high luster, without pits (indentations) or blemishes. However, a smooth and flawless specimen is exceptional. Most pearls fall into the categories of very good, average, fair, and imperfect, and, although there is no official industrywide certification system for pearls, they are often assigned a general value, which ranks them by their surface: "VVS" (very, very slightly spotted), "VS," "SI," and "Imperfect."

UNIFORMITY A particularly important consideration when buying pearl jewelry is uniformity. The closer the match in all of the categories, the more valuable the piece of jewelry. It can take years to match natural pearls. Today, it is fashionable to mix colors in a single necklace, such as black, gray, and white; or to combine different shades of the same color, whether it is white, cream, gray, orange, pink, or mauve. While the colors in these new pieces are not matched, the pearls' tonal quality may be the same.

How to Care for a Pearl

The oldest pearl of record makes its current home in the Louvre Museum in Paris. The Hanoverian pearls coveted by Elizabeth I in the sixteenth century, while no longer intact as six long ropes, survive in jewels worn today by the British royal family. Several well-known pearl purchases have taken very different forms but, thanks to a little effort, continue to adorn owner after owner within the same family or without. The famous $1.2 million double-strand necklace of 55 and 73 natural pearls, weighing a total of 1,712 grains—the first pearls ever to be offered at such a price—was traded by Louis Cartier in 1917, in exchange for the residence of New York banker Morton Plant. To this day, the mansion houses Cartier's U.S. headquarters on Fifth Avenue, but competition from cultured pearls reduced the value of natural pearls, and Maisie Plant's necklace brought only $157,000 when, after her death in 1957, the strands were sold at auction at Parke-Bernet Galleries (now Sotheby's). In the case of Catherine the Great's million-dollar pearls, which Detroit's Horace Dodge bought from Cartier for his wife, Anna Dodge's attention to maintenance preserved the pearls until her granddaughter destroyed the necklace and their historical value. "She asked for the pearls as an advance on her inheritance," says Dodge's great-grandson, Robert Petz. "One day, deciding to spread the wealth, she cut up the necklace and gave the perfectly matched pearls away, one by one. My great-grandmother kept them in a customized, walk-in jewelry safe in her bedroom wall, which required two people to open (one for the vault, one for the alarm in another room), and she wore them all the time to retain their luster."

TO WEAR OR NOT TO WEAR YOUR PEARLS The first rule of guardianship is that pearls should be the last thing you put on before you leave your home and the first thing you take off when you return. In other words, put your pearls on after you have applied makeup, hair spray, and fragrance; this caution will help you to avoid some of the accidents that can damage your pearls. As sturdy as their round form appears, pearls are actually about as strong as a fingernail, and their crystalline construction and lustrous surface are much more fragile than those of other gems. Pearls are soft. They are also alkaline, which means that their natural enemies are acids: our favorite beauty products, including perfume, eau de toilette, cosmetics, and hair spray; the

The fabled egg-shaped La Régente pearl of 337 grains (84.25 carats), which empress Marie-Louise wore on her tiara. It was worn later by Empress Eugénie and eventually by Russia's Princess Zenaïde Youssoupov. The prized pearl disappeared after the Russian Revolution. The pearl resurfaced for sale by Christie's in Geneva in May 1998. Most recently, New York's Fred Leighton sold the pearl to an Arab family.

chlorine in swimming pools; vinegar (even those delicious vinaigrette dressings); ink; body oils or perspiration, and less obvious adversaries, such as the bleach and ammonia contained in many ordinary household and jewelry cleaners. Avoid contact with these substances, as they will spot or eat away at your pearls. Don't use commercial jewelry cleaners or those wonderful ultrasonic cleaners in the dentist's office that revitalize your diamond rings. Take off your pearls before exercising or swimming. And be careful of spills and splashes when eating foods such as salad dressing, cleaning windows and glass tables, doing the laundry, and writing letters.

THE CLEANING SOLUTION   The simplest way to clean pearls is to wipe them with a soft cloth—a jeweler's cloth, a soft towel, a cotton T-shirt, or the like. Always wipe your pearls carefully with a dry cloth after each wearing. Periodically, and especially if a damaging substance has splashed against your jewelry, wipe your pearls with a cloth dampened with warm water. Some jewelers suggest washing pearls with warm, soapy water (milled or bar soap, not detergent) and patting them dry in a fluffy towel. Other experts insist that washing will weaken the cords, and recommend that strands be washed only when they are restrung. New York costume jeweler Clive Kandel reminisces about the cleaning solution that the premier pearl dealer Leonard Rosenthal suggested to his friend the rani of Pudukota (from southern India) while dining at the Ritz Hotel in Paris during the 1920s: "He told her to soak her spectacular pearl necklace—a single strand of 12 mm pearls—in a bottle filled with a solution of olive oil and ether. You couldn't do that today. But her pearls were well preserved, and after her death, her son wore them under his clothes until he died in the late 1980s."

Remember that despite their need for proper care, pearls also deserve to be enjoyed. One of New Orleans' grandes dames, Chico Pipes, who was born and raised in prerevolutionary Cuba, recalls her mother and her mother's friends taking their annual swim in the Havana harbor, which is known as the String of Pearls. "They went in with hats and veils and covered with pearls," she chuckles. "Swimming under the bridge so as not to get a suntan, they would just float around like frogs full of jewelry—just giving their pearls a wash." Chico says that Cuban families invested a lot of money in jewelry, and there were innumerable pearls in Cuban history. "Cuba is called the Pearl of the Antilles," she says. When her father died, Chico's four daughters combined their pearl inheritance into a bold pearl bracelet which they presented to her as a gift "from the girls and their father."

PROPER STORAGE   In order to keep pearls from scratching, store them by them-selves in a clean, soft pouch or a separate section of a jewelry box. An alternative is to wrap your pearls in a linen hand towel or handkerchief, a cotton T-shirt, or even a facial tissue. The idea is to use containers that are porous. Pearls need the moisture in the air to maintain their luster, which means that a safety-deposit box or vault is the least friendly environment. If you must keep your pearls under lock in these dark, dry con-tainers, periodically wipe them with a damp cloth.

LONG-TERM MAINTENANCE   Restringing pearl necklaces is vital to their long-term health. It keeps your pearls looking their best, and it is a safety precaution. If you wear them all the time, have them restrung on an annual basis. For lighter wear, a restringing every two years is perfectly fine. New York's Margaret Hoisik learned her craft at Tiffany and has been stringing pearls for forty-five years. In her windowed cubby at Albert Pujol in Manhattan, Hoisik demonstrates the process: She cuts a string of pearls apart, putting them, one by one, in a wooden tray to keep them in order (a piece of velvet would also work). She "tips" a length of silk thread by dip-ping it into melted gum arabic, which then hardens into a needlelike point. Using the point, she guides the thread through each pearl until a section of pearls is in place, and then she ties the knots. She repeats the process until all the pearls are strung. Hoisik uses a tiny piece of wire to attach the strand to the clasp.

The knots between each pearl not only prevent the pearls from colliding and scratching one another but prevent total chaos when a string breaks at the wrong time. Professionals also prefer silk thread because it is both fine and strong. Seed pearls, the sole exception, are just too small to knot. It is easy to tell when your pearls are ready for restringing—the knots look dirty, and the string has stretched, leaving unsightly gaps between the pearls. After proper storage, cleaning, and restringing, the best way to maintain your pearls is to wear them. They thrive on the combination of oil and water—the natural oils from you skin and the moisture in the air.

LUSTRE

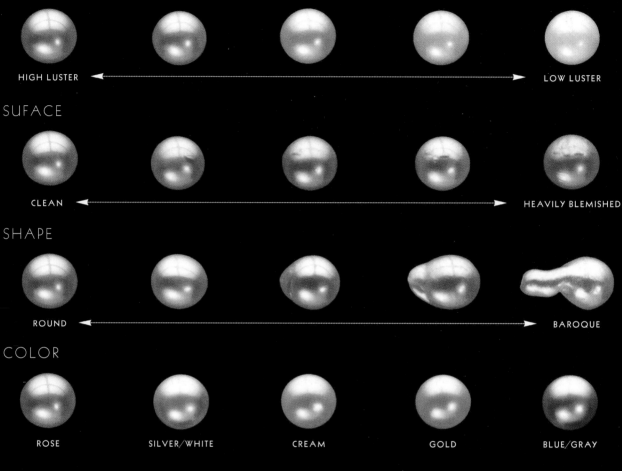

HIGH LUSTER ←--→ LOW LUSTER

SUFACE

CLEAN ←--→ HEAVILY BLEMISHED

SHAPE

ROUND ←--→ BAROQUE

COLOR

ROSE   SILVER/WHITE   CREAM   GOLD   BLUE/GRAY

SIZE

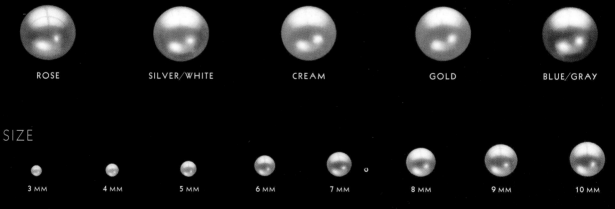

3 MM   4 MM   5 MM   6 MM   7 MM   8 MM   9 MM   10 MM

A Primer on the Different Pearl Varieties

ABALONE: The ear-shaped (ormer) abalone sea creature produces a small, highly iridescent baroque pearl that is prized by collectors for its color and rarity. The abalone is also sought for its mother-of-pearl shell and its meat.

AKOYA: Akoya, also known as Japanese pearls, have been synonymous with cultured pearls since the 1950s. Named for the Akoya oyster (*Pinctada fucata*) from Japan's Ago Bay, these pearls have accounted traditionally for most of the world's supply of cultured pearls. Akoya pearls range in size from 2 mm to 10 mm in diameter and develop in a range of shapes, from round to irregular. They are noted for their high luster and rich colors, which vary from white and cream to gray, blue, green, gold, silver, and pink.

BIWA PEARLS: These cultured freshwater pearls named for Japan's Lake Biwa region were introduced in the 1930s as a follow-up to what the Japanese had achieved with cultured seawater pearls. The mussel used for breeding is larger than the seawater Akoya oyster and can accommodate more mantles, some producing crops of as many as twenty to thirty small pearls. Today, very few genuine Biwa pearls are produced in Japan, but cultured freshwater pearls—many of them from China, and particularly those shaped like forks, crosses, bars, and coins—are often referred to as Biwas.

BLACK OR TAHITIAN: Black pearls, known more commonly as Tahitian pearls, are cultivated by the black-lipped *Pinctada margaritifera* oyster in warm South Sea saltwater lagoons. Tahiti is known for its superior black pearls, although the mysterious spheres are also produced by fisheries in the Cook Islands and French Polynesia. They occur naturally in colors ranging from gray to almost black, with green, cobalt blue, rusty orange, or aubergine overtones, and they vary in size from 8 mm to 20 mm. The average size is 11 mm to 12 mm, and it can take as many as twelve harvest years to find enough black pearls—matching in size, shape, and color—to make a necklace.

BLISTER: These dome- and pear-shaped pearls are solid or hollow and grow against the mother-of-pearl lining of the mollusk. The mother-of-pearl border is retained from the shell lining when the pearl is removed. These pearls have an unusually high luster and a lovely iridescent surface.

BUTTON: Also known as *bouton* pearls, they are rounded but have a flat bottom, which gives them a buttonlike appearance.

CIRCLE OR RINGED: These round pearls have raised concentric circles or ridges that circle their surface.

CONCH: Like other pearls, the ones produced by these univalve sea creatures are made of calcium carbonate, but there is no buildup of layers of nacre. About one of every 15,000 conchs produces one of these nonnacreous pearls, which resemble coral beads and come in deep pink, lilac, or orange-pink colors. While some conch pearls are spherical, most come in small oval, teardrop, or button shapes.

HALF-PEARLS: Any pearl with a diameter of 2 mm to 3 mm that has been cut in half for use as border decoration is referred to as a half-pearl.

KESHI: Produced by accident in saltwater oysters, keshis are baroque pearls of solid nacre that grow right along with a cultured pearl. They range in size from the tiniest Japanese seed-sized specimens to South Sea varieties that reach up to 8 mm to 10 mm. Necklaces of twenty to as many as a hundred strands of the tiny variety were once popular, and today, despite a diminishing supply, there is a great deal of interest in the lustrous baroque South Sea keshis in colors ranging from white and cream to black, gold, yellow, mauve, and lilac.

MABÉ: These pearls are domed in round or pear shapes produced when a hemispherical piece of plastic is placed against the side of the shell interior. After the mollusk coats the dome with nacre, the pearl is removed from the shell, the plastic is taken away, and the remaining hollow is filled with epoxy. Finally, a backing of mother-of-pearl is secured to the assembled product. Commonly used for earrings, mabé pearls are more fragile than solid blister pearls and should be handled with some care, as they can easily crack or peel.

ORIENTAL: This name was formerly used to describe natural pearls from the *Pinctada radiata,* found in the Persian Gulf, the Red Sea, and the waters around Ceylon (now Sri Lanka). The name reflects the lustrous nature of pearls and also incorporates Marco Polo's description of the jewels he saw in his travels through the Orient.

Seed: These diminutive round natural pearls are usually less than 2 mm in size and weigh up to 0.5 grain. They are produced by both freshwater and saltwater mollusks. China's pearling industry produces plentiful quantities of small kernel-shaped pearls, dubbed "Rice Krispies." Many of the small irregular seed pearls are used in collar and choker necklaces, which are especially popular today in shades of lavender, blue, pink, apricot, brown, and peach.

South Sea: South Sea pearls start at 8 mm in diameter and can reach the rare but eye-popping size of 23 mm, the equivalent of a large gumball. The average size of today's South Sea pearl is 11 mm to 14 mm. Found originally in Indonesia during the 1920s, these noble specimens are produced by the silver-lipped *Pinctada maxima* saltwater oyster, the largest species of saltwater oyster, which is also found in Australia, the Philippines, Japan, and Myanmar (formerly Burma). Australia's Nicholas Paspaley is the largest and most successful producer of South Sea pearls. Burma was once the most important producer, and some experts insist that the original pinkish-white Burmese South Sea pearl, with its silky luster, is far superior in color and luster to the somewhat larger Australian variety favored in the 1990s. South Sea pearls come in many colors, from warm pink-splashed white to the more common silver-white. True yellow and gold, from the golden-lipped *Pinctada maxima,* are in great demand. South Sea pearls are cultivated for longer periods, have thicker nacre coatings than other pearls, and have the longest life expectancy of any cultured pearl.

Three-Quarter Pearls: Natural or cultured, these pearls are not fully round but give the impression of being round. They are suitable for mounted jewelry.

A Short Glossary of Pearl Terms

CONCHIOLIN—The brown, porous substance secreted by a mollusk that binds the layers of nacre together to form a pearl.

CULTIVATED PEARL—Another term for a cultured pearl.

FRESHWATER PEARL—Pearls produced by freshwater mollusks

GRAIN—The traditional standard of weight used for natural pearls, which has now been replaced by carat weight. One grain is equal to 0.002083 ounce or 0.0648 gram. There are 400 grains per ounce, 15.43 grains per gram, and 4 grains per carat.

IRIDESCENCE—The orient or rainbow effect on the surface, or just below the surface, of a pearl.

LUSTER—The rich glow that emanates from the center of a pearl.

MANTLE—The thick skin that encompasses the body of a mollusk and produces the substances that form both the shell and the pearl.

MOLLUSK—A shellfish or soft-bodied invertebrate that lives in a shell. Pearl-producing mollusks are primarily oysters, mussels, and conch.

MOTHER-OF-PEARL—The smooth, iridescent lining of the mollusk's shell that is also made of nacre.

MILLIMETER—The unit of measure used to determine the diameter of a pearl. One millimeter is equivalent to approximately 0.04 inch.

MOMME—The Japanese weight measurement used for pearls. One momme is equivalent to 3.75 grams, or 18.75 carats.

NACRE—The crystalline substance that the mollusk produces to surround an intruder in its shell. The overlapping layers of this combination of calcium carbonate or aragonite platelets that are bound with conchiolin, refracts light and produce the iridescence, while the build-up of layers creates pearl. The mother-of-pearl lining of the mollusk shell is the same nacreous material. (FYI: Pearls are almost 90 percent calcium carbonate, which is the main ingredient in Tums.)

NUCLEUS—The material that is placed surgically within the soft tissue of a mollusk and acts as an irritant which triggers the production of conchiolin, nacre, and, ultimately, a pearl.

ORIENT—The iridescent play of color on or just below the surface of a pearl, which is produced by the refraction and reflection of light among the crystals of nacre.

ORIENTAL PEARL—The name used formerly to indicate pearls from the Middle East. Along with other terms, such as "fine" and "wild," Oriental is another word for a natural pearl.

PEARL—The nacreous gem that is formed within a mollusk's shell as a natural reaction to an intruding irritant.

Shopping for Pearls

DESIGNERS AND JEWELERS THE WORLD OVER

Australia

MAKERS MARK GALLERY
85 Collins Street
Melbourne
tel: 61 3 9654 8488
(fine jewelry)
Gallery works with neighboring jeweler Altmann and Cheny for pearl enhancers, clasps, and other jewelry of Australian gemstones.

PASPALEY PEARLS
142 King Street
Sydney, New South Wales 2000
tel: 61 2 9232 7633
(fine jewelry)

China

ADLER JEWELRY LIMITED
Mandarin Oriental Hotel
Shop M5, Mezzanine Floor
5 Conaught Road
Central Hong Kong
tel: 852 2366 6616
fax: 852 2722 7334
(fine jewelry)

K. S. SZE & SONS
M-11 Mandarin Oriental Hotel
Hong Kong
tel: 852 2524 2803
fax: 852 2526 0927
(fine jewelry)

PO KWONG
184 Hong Kong Diamond
    Exchange Building
Duddell Street, Central
Hong Kong, China
tel: 852 2521 4686
(fine jewelry)

TRIO PEARL
M-10 Peninsula Hotel
Hong Kong
tel: 852 2367 9171
fax: 852 2369 7385
(fine jewelry)

Denmark

GEORG JENSEN
4 Amagertorv
DK-1160 Copenhagen K
tel: 45 38 14 48 48
(fine jewelry)

England

ASPREY & GARRARD
167 New Bond Street
London W1Y 0AR
tel: 44 171 493 6767
fax: 44 171 491 0384
(fine jewelry)
Also at the Dorchester hotel.

BOODLE & DUNTHORNE LTD.
1 Sloane Street
London SW1X 9LA
tel: 44 171 235 0111
(fine jewelry)

BUTLER & WILSON
189 Fulham Road
London SW3 6JN
tel: 44 171 352 3045
(costume jewelry)

CIRO PEARLS LTD.
61a Brompton Road
London SW3 1DP
tel: 44 171 589 5584
fax: 44 171 409 0673
(fine and costume jewelry)

COBRA & BELLAMY
149 Sloane Street
London SW1X 9BZ
tel: 44 171 730 2823
(fine and costume jewelry)

DE VROOMEN
20–22 Rosebery Avenue
London EC1R 4SX
tel: 44 171 837 4914
(fine jewelry)

ELIZABETH GAGE
20 Albemarle Street
London W1X 4LB
tel: 44 171 499 2879
fax: 44 171 495 4550
(fine jewelry)

HARRODS
Brompton Road
Knightsbridge
London SW1X 7XL
tel: 44 171 730 1234
(fine and costume jewelry)

MOUSSAIESS JEWELERS
The London Hilton
22 Park Lane
London, W1A 2HH
tel: 44 171 408 0487
(fine jewelry)

ROSE FINE JEWELS
15 Burlington Arcade
London W1V 9AB
tel: 44 171 493 4466
(fine jewelry)

STEINBERG & TOLKIEN
193 King's Road, Chelsea,
London SW3 5EB
tel: 44 171 376 3660
fax: 44 171 376 3630
(costume jewelry)

TESSIERS LTD.
26 New Bond Street
London W1Y 0JY
tel: 44 171 629 0458
(fine and estate jewelry)

THEO FENNELL PLC
169 Fulham Road
London SW3 6SP
tel: 44 171 591 5000
(fine jewelry)

WARTSKI LTD.
14 Grafton Street
London W1X 4DE
tel: 44 171 493 1141
(fine and estate jewelry)

France

BOUCHERON
26 Place Vendôme
75001 Paris
tel: 33 1 42 61 58 16
(fine jewelry)

BURMA
16 Rue de la Paix
75002 Paris
tel: 33 1 42 61 60 64
(costume jewelry)

CARTIER
7 Place Vendôme
75001 Paris
tel: 33 1 44 55 32 50
(fine jewelry)

CHAUMET
12 Place Vendôme
75001 Paris
tel: 33 1 44 77 24 00
fax: 33 1 42 60 41 44
(fine jewelry)

FRED
7 Place Vendôme
75001 Paris
tel: 33 1 42 86 60 60
fax: 33 1 42 86 60 59
(fine jewelry)

GALERIES LAFAYETTE
12 Place Grenette
38000 Grenoble
tel: 33 476 87 63 62
fax: 33 476 43 07 02
(fine and costume jewelry)

IBU POILANE
51 Rue de Varenne
75007 Paris
tel: 33 1 44 39 26 62
fax: 33 1 42 22 16 51
(fine jewelry)

JAR
7 Place Vendôme
75001 Paris
tel: 33 1 42 96 33 66
fax: 33 1 42 86 05 32
(fine jewelry)

MAUBOUSSIN
20 Place Vendôme
75001 Paris
tel: 33 1 44 55 10 00
fax: 33 1 44 55 10 09
(fine jewelry)

O. J. PERRIN
8 Rue de la Paix
75002 Paris
tel: 33 1 42 92 08 88
fax: 33 1 42 92 08 82
(fine jewelry)

POGGI
10 Rue de Grenelle
75006 Paris
tel: 33 1 45 48 11 28
(fashion jewelry)

VAN CLEEF & ARPELS
22 Place Vendôme
75001 Paris
tel: 33 1 53 45 45 45
fax: 33 1 53 45 45 00
(fine jewelry)

Germany

DARGO
Unter der Linden 77
Berlin
tel: 49 30 22 67 93 26
(fine jewelry)

HEMMERLE JUWELIERE
Maximilianstrasse 14
Munich
tel: 49 89 242 2600
(fine jewelry)

**KADEWE A.K.A. KAUFHAUS
DES WESTENS**
Tauentzienstrasse 21–24
Berlin
tel: 49 30 21 210
(fine, fashion, and costume
jewelry)

RIO
Bleibtreustrasse 52
Berlin
tel: 49 30 3133 152
(costume jewelry)

India

GEM PALACE
M. I. Road
Jaipur 302 011
tel: 91 141 374 175
fax: 91 141 373 586
(fine jewelry)

VIREN BHAGAT
4 Om Chambers
Kemps Corner
Mumbai 400 026
tel: 91 22 364 1905
fax: 91 22 363 7751
(fine jewelry)

Italy

BOZART
Via Bocca di Leone 4
Rome
tel: 39 06 6781026
(costume jewelry)

BUCCELLATI
Via Monte Napoleone 12
Milan
tel: 39 02 799 944
(fine jewelry)
Also in Rome and Paris

BULGARI
Via Condotti 10
Rome
tel: 39 06 6793876
(fine jewelry)

DELLA LOGGIA
Ponte Vecchio 52/R
Florence
tel: 39 055 239 6028
(fine and estate jewelry)

TIFFANY-FARAONE
Via Tornabuoni 25/R
Florence
tel: 39 055 215 506
(fine jewelry)

STEFAN HAFNER
Via Vallestura 12–2
Bologna
tel: 39 051 580 590
(fine jewelry)

Japan

ANSHINDO CO. LTD.
43 Yokouchi-cho, Shizucka-shi,
Shizucka-Ken 420
fax: 81 54 247 6651
(fine jewelry)

MIKIMOTO
5-5, 4-chome, Ginza, Chuo-ku
Tokyo 104
tel: 81 3 3535 4611
(fine jewelry)

TASAKI SHINJU PEARL GALLERY
1–3–3 Akasaka, Minato-ku
tel: 81 3 5561 8881
fax: 81 3 5562 9271
(fine jewelry)

YAMAKATSU PEARL CO.
Toranomon Yamakatsu Building
1–40,Toranomon 4-chome,
Minato-ku,
Tokyo 105
tel: 81 3 3437 3311
(fine jewelry)

Scotland

HAMILTON & INCHES LTD.
87 George Street
Edinburgh EH23EY
tel: 44 131 225 4898
(fine and costume jewelry)

Switzerland

D. GALLOPIN & CIE
1 Place des Bergues
Case Postale 1600
1211 Geneva 1
tel: 41 22 716 2 716
(fine jewelry)

United States

AZEVEDO
210 Post Street
San Francisco, CA 94108
tel: 1-415-781-0063
fax: 1-415-781-2813
(fine jewelry)

CYNTHIA WOLFF
Los Angeles, CA
tel: 1-310-395-9533
fax: 1-310-393-9594
(fine jewelry)

DAVID ORGELL
320 North Rodeo Drive
Beverly Hills, CA 90210
tel: 1-310-273-6660
(fine jewelry)

ERICA COURTNEY
7465 Beverly Boulevard
Los Angeles, CA 90036
tel: 1-323-938-2373
(fine jewelry)

GUMPS
135 Post Street
San Francisco, CA 94108
tel: 1-415-982-1616
fax: 1-415-984-9379
(fine and estate jewelry)

HILARY BEANE
(showroom only)
Los Angeles, CA
tel: 1-213-891-0062
fax: 1-213-891-0067
(fine jewelry)
Available at Neiman Marcus and
Bergdorf Goodman, among others.

HAWAII TAHITI PEARLS
2255 Kuhio Avenue, Suite 1001
Honolulu, HI 96815
tel: 1-808-923-6797
(fine jewelry)

EVE ALFILLE GALLERY
623 Grove Street
Evanston, IL 60201
tel: 1-847-869-7920
(fashion jewelry)

BORSHEIM'S
120 Regency Parkway
Omaha, NE 68114
tel: 1-402-391-0400
fax: 1-402-391-6694
(fine jewelry)

LUNA FELIX GALLERY
116 West San Francisco Street
Santa Fe, NM 87501
tel: 1-505-989-7679
(fine jewelry)

A LA VIEILLE RUSSIE
at The Sherry Netherland Hotel
785 Fifth Avenue
New York, NY 10022
tel: 1-212-752-1727
(fine and estate jewelry)

ANGELA CUMMINGS
(by appointment only)
730 Fifth Avenue
New York, NY 10019
tel: 1-212-757-7841
(fine jewelry)

ANN CRABTREE
1310 Madison Avenue
New York, NY 10128
tel: 1-212-996-6499
fax: 1-212-996-5641
(fashion jewelry)
Also in East Hampton.

ASPREY & GARRARD
725 Fifth Avenue
New York, NY 10022
tel: 1-212-688-1811
fax: 1-212-826-3746
(fine and estate jewelry)

BARNEYS
Madison Avenue at 61st Street
New York, NY 10021
tel: 1-212-826-8900
fax: 1-212-833-2018
(fine and fashion jewelry, including
designs by Linda Lee Johnson,
Renee Lewis, Gabrielle Sanchez,
Sharon Aluof, Gurhan Orhan,
Kazuko Oshima, and Suzanne Bell)

BERGDORF GOODMAN
754 Fifth Avenue
New York, NY 10022
tel: 1-212-753-7300
fax: 1-212-872-8716
(fine, estate, and costume
jewelry)

BLOOMINGDALE'S
1000 Third Avenue
New York, NY 10022
tel: 1-212-705-2000
(fine, fashion, and costume
jewelry)

BOUCHERON JOAILLERIE
460 Park Avenue, 12th lloor
New York, NY 10022
tel: 1-212-715-7330
fax: 1-212-715-7379
(fine jewelry)

BUCCELLATI
46 East 57th Street
New York, NY 10022
tel: 1-212-308-2900
(fine jewelry)
Also in Beverly Hills.

CAROLEE DESIGNS
(wholesale showroom)
385 Fifth Avenue
New York, NY 10001
tel: 1-212-689-4409
fax: 1-212-689-0165
(costume and fashion jewelry)
Available at Saks Fifth Avenue,
Bloomingdale's, Harrods, Neiman
Marcus, and Mitsukoshi.

CARTIER
653 Fifth Avenue
New York, NY 10022
tel: 1-212-753-0111
(fine jewelry)
Also in Beverly Hills, San Diego,
San Francisco, Bal Harbour, Boca
Raton, Palm Beach, Atlanta, Hon-
olulu, Chicago, Chevy Chase,
Boston, St. Louis, Las Vegas, San
Juan, Dallas, Houston, Vancouver,
Toronto, and Montreal

CELLINI
509 Madison Avenue
New York, NY 10022
tel: 1-212-754-6240
fax: 1-212-888-0505
(fine jewelry)

CHANEL
15 East 57th Street
New York, NY 10020
tel: 1-212-355-5050
fax: 1-212-715-4150
(fine and costume jewelry)

CHRISTIAN DIOR
712 Fifth Avenue
New York, NY 10019
tel: 1-212-582-0500
fax: 1-212-582-1063
(costume jewelry)

CHRISTOPHER WALLING
(by appointment only)
608 Fifth Avenue, 7th floor
New York, NY 10019
tel: 1-212-581-7700
fax: 1-212-581-1117
(fine jewelry)

CINER
(wholesale showroom)
20 West 37th Street, 10th floor
New York, NY 10018
tel: 1-212-947-3770
fax: 1-212-643-0357
(costume jewelry)

CLIVE KANDEL
(by appointment only)
645 Madison Avenue, Room 1703
New York, NY 10021
tel: 1-212-750-5379
fax: 1-212-750-5426
(costume jewelry)

DAVID BIRNBAUM
(by appointment only)
22 West 48th Street, 11th floor
New York, NY 10036
tel: 1-212-575-0267
fax: 1-212-398-9438
(fine jewelry)

DAVID WEBB
445 Park Avenue
New York, NY 10022
tel: 1-212-421-3030
(fine jewelry)

ELIZABETH LOCKE
968 Madison Avenue
New York, NY 10021
tel: 1-212-744-7878
fax: 1-212-744-5565
(fine jewelry)

ELLA GEM
(by appointment only)
580 Fifth Avenue, Suite 3110
New York, NY 10036
tel: 1-212-398-0101
fax: 1-212-302-0153
(fine jewelry)

ERICKSON-BEAMON
(showroom)
498 Seventh Avenue, 24th floor
New York, NY 10018
tel: 1-212-971-6006
fax: 1-212-971-6066
(fashion jewelry)

FRAGMENTS
107 Greene Street
New York, NY 10013
tel: 1-212-334-9588
tel: 1-212-226-8878 (wholesale)
(fine, fashion, and costume
jewelry)
Representing Wendy Brigode,
Cynthia Wolff, Cynthia Meyer,
and Dana Kellin, among others.

**FRED LEIGHTON RARE
COLLECTIBLE JEWELS**
773 Madison Avenue
New York, NY 10021
tel: 1-212-288-1872
fax: 1-212-288-6167
(fine jewelry)
Also at Via Bellagio in Las Vegas.

H. STERN JEWELERS
645 Fifth Avenue
New York, NY 10022-5910
tel: 1-212-688-0300
fax: 1-212-888-5137
(fine, fashion, and estate
jewelry)

HARRY WINSTON
718 Fifth Avenue
New York, NY 10019
tel: 1-212-245-2000
fax: 1-212-765-8809
(fine jewelry)
Also in Beverly Hills, Geneva,
Paris, and Tokyo.

HENRI BENDEL
712 Fifth Avenue
New York, NY 10022
tel: 1-212-247-1100
(fashion jewelry)

HENRY DUNAY
(by appointment only)
22 West 48th Street
New York, NY 10036
tel: 1-212-768-9700
fax: 1-212-944-0308
(fine jewelry)
Available at Neiman Marcus, Gallopin et Cie, Georg Jensen, Adler
Jewelers, Anshindo, Dargo, and
McCarver & Moser.

ILIAS LALAOUNIS
733 Madison Avenue
New York, NY 10021
tel: 1-212-439-9400
fax: 1-212-439-9403
(fine jewelry)

KENNETH JAY LANE
(by appointment only)
20 West 37th Street
New York, NY 10018
tel: 1-212-868-1780
(costume jewelry)

KWM EXCLUSIVES
117 East 77th Street
New York, NY 10021
tel: 1-212-570-6065
(fine jewelry)

M & J SAVITT
(by appointment only)
475 Fifth Avenue
New York, NY 10017
tel: 1-212-684-4221
(fine jewelry)

MAJORICA PEARLS
366 Fifth Avenue
New York, NY 10001
tel: 1-212-695-1756
(costume jewelry)

MARINA B
809 Madison Avenue
New York, NY 10021
tel: 1-212-288-9708
(fine jewelry)

McCarver & Moser
27 Main Street
East Hampton, NY 11937
tel: 1-516-324-7300
fax: 1-516-324-0080
(fine jewelry)
Also in Sarasota.

Me & Ro
271 Lafayette Street
New York, NY 10012
tel: 1-212-431-8744
(fine jewelry)

Mikimoto
730 Fifth Avenue
New York, NY 10022
tel: 1-212-664-1800
(fine jewelry)
Also in London, Paris,
and Costa Mesa, California.

Mish
22 East 72nd Street, Suite 3B
New York, NY 10021
tel: 1-212-734-3500
fax: 1-212-734-0330
(fine and fashion jewelry)

Noa
110 Greene Street
New York, NY 10013
tel: 1-212-965-9000
fax: 1-212-941-5935
(fine and fashion jewelry)

Ralph Esmerian
(by appointment only)
610 Fifth Avenue, Room 414
New York, NY 10019
tel: 1-212-247-2944
fax: 1-212-582-6954
(fine and estate jewelry)

Raymond C. Yard
(by appointment only)
630 Fifth Avenue
New York, NY 10111
tel: 1-212-247-6222
fax: 1-212-397-2328
(fine jewelry)

Robert Lee Morris
400 West Broadway
New York, NY 10012
tel: 1-212-431-3630
fax: 1-212-219-9027
(fine jewelry)

Saks Fifth Avenue
630 Fifth Avenue
New York, NY 10022
tel: 1-212-753-4000
(fine, fashion, costume,
and estate jewelry)

Salvador Assael
(by appointment only)
580 Fifth Avenue
New York, NY 10036
tel: 1-212-819-0060
fax: 1-212-764-1965
(fine jewelry)

Seaman Schepps
485 Park Avenue
New York, NY 10022
tel: 1-212-753-9520
fax: 1-212-753-9531
(fine jewelry)

Ted Muehling
47 Greene Street
New York, NY 10013
tel: 1-212-431-3825
fax: 1-212-431-1754
(fine jewelry)

Tiffany & Co.
727 Fifth Avenue
New York, NY 10022
tel: 1-212-755-8000
(fine jewelry, including collections
by designers Paloma Picasso, Elsa
Peretti, and Jean Schlumberger)

Tourneau
12 East 57th Street
New York, NY 10022
tel: 1-212-758-7300
(fine jewelry)

Verdura
745 Fifth Avenue, Suite 1205
New York, NY 10022
tel: 1-212-265-3227
fax: 1-212-753-2395
(fine jewelry)
Neiman Marcus

Neiman Marcus
One Marcus Square
Dallas, TX 75201
tel: 1-214-363-8311
(fine, fashion, and costume jewelry)

Auction Houses

Christie's
502 Park Avenue
New York, NY 10022
tel: 1-212-636-2000

Guernsey's
108 East 73rd Street
New York, NY 10021
tel: 1-212-794-2280
fax: 1-212 794-3638
fax: 1-212-794-2286

Phillip's
406 East 79th Street
New York, NY 10021
tel: 1-212-570-4830
fax: 1-212-570-2207

Sotheby's
1334 York Avenue
New York, NY 10021
tel: 1-212-606-7392

William Doyle Galleries
175 East 87th Street
New York, NY 10128
tel: 1-212-427-2730

Online

Please note: Although there are
exceptions, to date, online
resources are generally best for
inexpensive pearls. Here are some
that were available at the time this
book went to print.

www.adornis.com

www.ashford.com

www.bluenile.com

www.buyjewel.com

www.carolee.com

www.erwinpearl.com

www.firstjewelry.com

www.fond-tanagra.com

www.iqvc.com

www.miadora.com

www.mondera.com

www.luxuryfinder.com

www.paspaleypearls.com

Photo Credits

Endpapers: Photograph by Stephanie Pfriender. Courtesy of the photographer

page i: Kiki de Montparnasse in the film *L'Étoile de Mer*, 1928. Photograph by Man Ray. Courtesy of Janet Lehr Inc., New York, and the Man Ray Trust

pages ii–iii: Chanel ready-to-wear spring-summer 1995. Modeled by Brandy. Photograph by Karl Lagerfeld. © Karl Lagerfeld. Courtesy of Chanel

page vi: Uma Thurman, 1996. Photograph by Annie Leibovitz. Courtesy Contact Press Images

page x: Pearls by Ibu Poilane. Courtesy of the designer

page xiii: (left to right) Anna Wintour, Princess Diana, Hillary Clinton, 1996. Courtesy of AP/Wide World Photos

A Quirk of Nature

page 2: Claudette Colbert as Cleopatra, 1934. Courtesy of Photofest

page 6: White Party at the Vizcaya Museum and Gardens, Miami, 1996. Photograph by Cindy Karp. Courtesy of the photographer and *The New York Times*

page 7: Daryl Hannah, New York, 1989. Photograph by Harry Benson. Courtesy of the photographer

page 8: French Nude. Courtesy of Philippe Garner

page 9: Henry Cyril Paget, 5th Marquis of Anglesey, early 1900s. Postcard photograph, possibly by John Wickens. Courtesy of the National Trust Photographic Library, London

page 10: Kiki de Montparnasse. Photograph by Man Ray. Copyright © Man Ray Trust, ARS, New York. Courtesy of Timothy Baum, New York

page 11: Mrs. Leo (Edwina) D'Erlanger, 1949. Photograph by Cecil Beaton. Courtesy of Sotheby's London

page 12: Elizabeth Taylor. Photo by Liza Todd. Courtesy of Liza Todd and Christopher Walling

page 13: *Girl with a Pearl Earring*, ca. 1665–1666. Painting by Jan Vermeer. Royal Cabinet of Paintings, Mauritshuis, The Hague

page 15: Isabella Stewart Gardner in Venice, 1894. Painting by Anders Leonard Zorn. Courtesy of the Isabella Stewart Gardner Museum

page 16: Princess Gloria von Thurn und Taxis, 1987. Photograph by Robert Mapplethorpe. Copyright © the Estate of Robert Mapplethorpe. Used with permission

page 19: Carrie Donovan, 1997. Photograph by Jesse Frohman. © Jesse Frohman. Courtesy of Old Navy

Innocents

page 20: Grand Duchess Anastasia of Russia, daughter of Czar Nicholas, as a young girl. Courtesy of Corbis-Bettmann

page 23: Jessica at five, 1987. Photograph by Sally Mann. Courtesy of Edwynn Houk Gallery, New York

page 24: Daughters of Nicholas II, czar of Russia. Courtesy of Corbis-Bettmann

page 26: (top) Ruth Elizabeth Brodie, ca. 1935. Courtesy of a private collection

page 26: (bottom) Caroline Buchanan Brodie, ca. 1950. Courtesy of a private collection

page 27: Barbara Hutton, 1915. Courtesy of Corbis-Bettmann

page 29: Elizabeth Taylor and Montgomery Clift in *A Place in the Sun,* 1951. Courtesy of the Academy of Motion Picture Arts and Sciences

page 30: Biarritz, France, August 1951. Photograph by Robert Capa. Courtesy of Magnum Photos, Inc.

page 31: Mrs. John Sims Kelly, former Brenda D. D. Frazier, lunches with her daughter at the Stork Club, ca. 1950–1951. Photograph by Jerome Zerbe

page 33: (top) Diane Goldman, engagement photo, 1929. Courtesy of private collection

page 33: (bottom) Sam and Diane Avirom, hand-tinted wedding photo, 1930. Courtesy of private collection

page 34: Countess Barbara von Reventlow, the former Barbara Hutton, Palm Beach, Florida, January 18, 1940. Courtesy of Corbis-Bettman

page 35: Countess Barbara von Reventlow, the former Barbara Hutton, with her Danish count, at Wimbledon, 1937. Courtesy of Corbis-Bettmann

page 37: Polly's wedding, May 1998. Photograph by Tina Barney. ©Tina Barney. Courtesy of Janet Borden Gallery, Inc.

page 38: E. Thomas Williams, Jr., and Auldlyn Higgins on their wedding day, Baltimore, Maryland, May 23, 1964. Courtesy of private collection

Lords & Lovers

page 40: *Elizabeth I, 1533–1603.* By or after George Gower, ca. 1588. Courtesy of the National Portrait Gallery, London

page 43: Princess Marie-Chantal of Greece. Photograph by David Seidner. © 1999 Estate of David Seidner. Courtesy of the Estate of David Seidner

page 44: The Princess of Berar, wife of the last Sultan of the Ottoman Empire, Hyderabad, March 1944. Photograph by Cecil Beaton. Courtesy of Sotheby's, London

page 46: Empress Hirohito. Courtesy of Kyodo News International, Inc., Tokyo page 48: *Henry VIII*. Painting by Hans Holbein. Courtesy of the Board of Trustees of the National Museums and Galleries of Merseyside, Walker Art Gallery, Liverpool, England

page 52: Elizabeth Taylor wearing La Peregrina at the premiere of *Little Foxes*, 1981. Courtesy of Sonia Moskowitz

page 53: *Queen Mary Tudor*, daughter of Catherine of Aragon, 1554. Painting by Hans Eworth. Courtesy of the National Portrait Gallery, London

page 56: Last maharajas. Courtesy of *The Last Maharajas*, 1981

page 57: His Highness Jam Sahib of Narajamer, October 1920. Photograph by Lafayette. Courtesy of the Victoria and Albert Museum, London

page 61: Grand duchesses in the Russian court, May 23, 1896. Courtesy of *The Last Courts of Europe: A Royal Family Album, 1860-1914*

page 62: Princess Alexandra, 1897. Courtesy of Culver Pictures

page 63: Olga de Meyer posing at Buckingham Palace in a Worth gown, ca. 1900. Photograph by Baron Adolph de Meyer. ©Estate of Baron de Meyer. Courtesy of the G. Ray Hawkins Gallery

page 65: Princess Eugénie in Oriental costume, before 1865. Hand-colored albumen print. Courtesy of Gilman Paper Company Collection

page 66: Contessa de Castiglione, ca. 1857. Courtesy of the Musée d'Unterlinden, Colmar

page 67: Marchesa Luisa Casati, 1912. Photograph by Baron Adolph de Meyer. Courtesy of private collection

page 69: Consuelo, duchess of Marlborough, with her two sons, the marquis of Blandford and Lord Ivor Spencer-Churchill, 1898. Photograph by Alice Hughes. Courtesy of Hugo Vickers Collection

page 71: Elizabeth and Philip on their wedding day, November 20, 1947. *Vogue*, January 1948. Courtesy *Vogue*, Condé Nast Publications, Inc.

page 71: Elizabeth's wedding dress, *The Illustrated London News*, November 22, 1947. Courtesy of *The Illustrated London News* Picture Library

page 72: *Queen Victoria*, 1899. Painting by Bertha Muller. Courtesy of the National Portrait Gallery, London

page 75: Elizabeth, the Queen Mother. Photograph by Dorothy Wilding. Courtesy of Camera Press, London

Traditionalists

page 76: Ronald and Nancy Reagan, Hollywood, mid-1950s. Courtesy of Corbis-Bettmann

page 78: Judy Garland. Courtesy of Neal Peters Collection

page 79: Helen Keller, Paris, France. Photograph by Werner Bischof. Courtesy of Magnum Photos, Inc.

page 79: Coretta Scott King. Photograph by Lawrence Fried. Courtesy of Magnum Photos, Inc.

page 80: Bert Williams. Courtesy of Yale University Collection of American Literature, Beinecke Rare Book and Manuscript Library, the James Weldon Johnson Papers

page 81: Mrs. William Hayden English Walling, 1946. Courtesy of Christopher Walling

page 83: Maria Callas, 1957. Photograph by Cecil Beaton. Courtesy of Sotheby's London

page 84: Lily Auchincloss. Photograph by John Hall. Courtesy of Alexandra Auchincloss

page 85: Tree family (from top clockwise: Penelope Tree, Frances FitzGerald, Marietta Tree, and Mrs. Peabody), 1979. Photograph by Lichfield. Courtesy of the photographer

page 86: "A Tribute to America's First Ladies," U.S. Botanic Garden, 1994. Photograph by Barbara Kinney. Courtesy of the White House and the National Archives

page 87: Barbara Bush, Washington, D.C., 1989. Photograph by Harry Benson. Courtesy of the photographer

page 89: C.Z. Guest in Mainbocher, 1951. Photograph by Louise Dahl Wolfe. Courtesy of F.I.T., New York

page 90: Homage to Henri Soulé's Le Pavillon at 5 East Fifty-Fifth Street, in New York City. Caught in a single day are, top row, the duchess of Windsor and the Marquesa Alfonso de Portago; middle row, the Viscountess Paul de Rosière and Alfred Hitchcock; bottom row, Mrs. John C. Wilson and Noël Coward, *Town & Country* cover, June 1956. Photograph by Luis Lemus. Courtesy of *Town & Country* magazine

page 93: Carolina Herrera, 1979. Photograph by Robert Mapplethorpe. Copyright © the Estate of Robert Mapplethorpe. Used with permission

page 94: Nan Kempner, Fran Stark, and Jacqueline de Ribes, the Metropolitan Opera 100th Anniversary Gala, New York City, 1984. Photograph by Roxanne Lowit. Courtesy of the photographer

page 95: Diane von Furstenberg. Photograph by Aufdembrinke/Schorr. Courtesy of Retna

page 97: Mrs. George C. Gould. Courtesy of Brown Brothers

page 98: Dolly Hoffman. Courtesy of private collection

page 99: Irene Castle, late 1920s. Photograph by Cecil Beaton. Courtesy of Sotheby's, London

page 100: Lady Diana Cooper, ca. 1925–1927. Photograph by Curtis Moffat. Courtesy of Hugo Vickers Collection

page 103: Kelly Klein, New York City, 1988. Photograph by Mary Hilliard. Courtesy of the photographer

page 103: The duke and duchess of Windsor, guests at the third annual spring festival at the Greenbrier, May 4, 1950. Courtesy of Corbis-Bettmann

page 105: Gertrude Vanderbilt Whitney in Bakst, 1912 Photograph by Baron Adolph de Meyer, *Vogue*, January 15, 1913 Courtesy *Vogue*, Condé Nast Publications, Inc.

page 107: Amelia Earhart, ca. 1920. Courtesy of Photofest.

page 111: Michele Oka Doner, 1999. Photograph by Sheila Metzner. Courtesy of the photographer

Dream Makers

page 112: Marlene Dietrich in "Desire," 1936. Courtesy of the Academy of Motion Picture Arts and Sciences

page 114: The Honorable Stephen Tennant as Prince Charming, 1927. Photograph by Cecil Beaton. Courtesy of Sotheby's, London

page 115: Rudolph Valentino in *The Young Rajah,* 1922. Courtesy of Neal Peters

page 116-117: Lillie Langtree as Mrs. Trevelyan, 1899. Photograph by Lafayette. Courtesy of the Victoria and Albert Museum, London

page 118: Héléna Christensen, spring-summer 1995 ready-to-wear collection. Photograph by Wolf Schuffner. Courtesy of Chanel

page 119: Coco Chanel and Serge Lifar. Photograph by Jean Morain. Courtesy of private collection

page 120: Milla Jovovich, spring-summer, 1998. fine jewelry and haute couture collections. Photograph by Karl Lagerfeld. ©Karl Lagerfeld for Chanel. Courtesy of Chanel

page 123: Diana Vreeland. Photograph by Evelyn Hofer. Courtesy of the photographer

page 127: Jeanne Toussaint, Paris, 1938. Photograph by Francois Kollar. Courtesy of the Patrimoine Photographie

page 128: Josephine Baker, ca. 1922. Photograph by Baron Adolph de Meyer. Courtesy of Robert Miller Gallery, New York. © G. Ray Hawkins, LA

page 129: Erté, Sporting Club, Monte Carlo, 1922. Courtesy of Sevenarts, London

page 131: Colette in the flat at 177-bis Rue de Courcelles. Courtesy of Anne de Jouvenal

page 132: (from left to right) Marilyn Monroe, Jack Lemmon, and Tony Curtis in *Some Like it Hot,* 1959. Courtesy of the Museum of Modern Art, Film Stills Department

page 133: Marilyn Monroe. Courtesy of Neal Peters Collection

page 134: Audrey Hepburn in *Breakfast at Tiffany's,* 1961. Courtesy of Photofest

page 136: Mary J. Blige, 1999. Photograph by Robert Maxwell. Courtesy of the photographer

page 137: Alla Nazimova from *Salome,* 1923. Courtesy of the Museum of Modern Art, Film Stills Department

page 138: Greta Garbo in *The Mysterious Lady,* 1928. Courtesy of Photofest

page 140: Sigourney Weaver, 1988. Photograph by Robert Mapplethorpe. Copyright © the Estate of Robert Mapplethorpe. Used with permission

page 141: Pearl headdress worn by Natalie Portman as Queen Amidala in the film *Star Wars: Episode I: The Phantom Menace,* 1999. Courtesy of Lucasfilm Ltd.

page 142: Tim Curry in *The Rocky Horror Picture Show,* 1975. Photograph by Mick Rock. Copyright © Mick Rock, 1974

page 143: Billy Boy, 1984. Photograph by Alice Springs. Courtesy of the photographer

page 144: Carol Burnett as Nora Desmond. Courtesy of CBS

page 146: Bette Davis and Errol Flynn in *The Private Lives of Elizabeth and Essex,* 1939. Courtesy of Photofest

page 147: Salma Hayek, 1999. Photograph by Matthew Rolston. Courtesy of the model and the photographer

page 148: Whoopi Goldberg dressed as Elizabeth at the 71st Academy Awards, 1998. Courtesy © Academy of Motion Picture Arts and Sciences

page 149: Detail of Whoopi Goldberg's costume worn at the Academy Awards presentation. Photograph by Gideon Lewin. Courtesy of the photographer

page 150: Mrs. Arturo Lopez at the Beistegui Ball, Venice, 1951. Photograph by Cecil Beaton. Courtesy of Sotheby's, London

page 151: Daisy, Princess of Pless, dressed as the Queen of Sheba for the Devonshire House Ball, 1897. Courtesy of the Victoria and Albert Museum

page 155: Marisa Berenson dressed as the Marchesa Luisa Casati for the Rothschild Proust Ball, 1971. Photograph by Cecil Beaton. Courtesy of Sotheby's, London

page 156: Mrs. Beaton, ca. 1925. Photograph by Cecil Beaton. Courtesy of Sotheby's, London

page 157: Cecil Beaton, 1925. Photograph by Dorothy Wilding. Courtesy of the National Portrait Gallery

Untouchables

page 158: Grace Kelly at the Cannes Film Festival, 1955. Photograph by Edward Quinn. © Edward Quinn/The Edward Quinn Archive, c/o Scalo Publishers, Zurich

page 161: Jacqueline Kennedy at the Jeu de Paume, Paris, June 2, 1961. Courtesy of Corbis-Bettmann

page 163: Princess Diana. Photograph by Lord Snowdon. Courtesy of Camera Press

page 164: Grace Kelly on her wedding day with Prince Rainier III of Monaco, 1956. Photograph by Howell Conant. Courtesy © Howell Conant/Bob Adelman Books from *Grace*

page 166: Grace Kelly at the Film Festival, Cannes, 1955. Photograph by Edward Quinn. © Edward Quinn/ The Edward Quinn Archive. Courtesy Scalo Publishers, Zurich

page 168: Princess Grace with Princess Caroline, Monaco, ca. 1964. Photograph by Howell Conant. Courtesy © Howell Conant/Bob Adelman Books from *Grace*

page 169: Princess Grace, Jamaica, 1955. Photograph by Howell Conant. Courtesy © Howell Conant/Bob Adelman Books from *Grace*

page 171: Jacqueline Bouvier on the day of her marriage to Massachussetts Senator John F. Kennedy, Newport, Rhode Island, September 12, 1953. Molly Thayer Collection, Courtesy of Magnum Photos, Inc.

page 173: Jacqueline Kennedy and her son, John F. Kennedy, Jr., upstairs in the White House. Courtesy of Gamma Liaison

page 174: Jacqueline Kennedy at the April in Paris Ball, New York, March 1955. Photograph by Slim Aarons. Courtesy of Tony Stone Images

page 175: Jacqueline Kennedy and Lee Radziwill in India. Photograph by Marilyn Silverstone. Courtesy of Magnum Photos

page 176: Diana, Ascot, June 1989. Photograph by Jayne Fincher. Courtesy of the photographer

page 178: Diana in Venice with her family, April 1985. Photograph by Jayne Fincher. Courtesy of the photographer

page 183: Diana and her sister, *Hello* magazine, April 18, 1998. Courtesy of London Features International Ltd.

Eternal Lights

page 184: C.Z. Guest, Palm Beach, Florida, 1989. Photograph by Bruce Weber. Courtesy of the photographer

page 186: C.Z. Guest and Chris Dunphy at the Polo Ball, Palm Beach, 1954. Courtesy of Archive Photos

page 187: C.Z. Guest and Mme. Jacques Balsan. Courtesy of Tony Stone Images

page 189: Mrs. Stanley Grafton Mortimer, Jr., *Vogue,* March 1, 1946. Photograph by Horst. Courtesy *Vogue,* Condé Nast Publications, Inc.

page 191: Louise Brooks, 1920s. Courtesy of Kobal

page 192: Jacqueline Bouvier, age 22, after winning *Vogue*'s Prix de Paris competition, August 15, 1951. Photograph by Richard Rutledge. Courtesy Vogue, Condé Nast Publications Inc.

page 195: Elsie Mendl (Elsie de Wolfe), 1938. Photograph by François Kollar. Courtesy of Patrimoine Photographique

page 197: Brooke Astor. Photograph by Anders Overgaard. Courtesy of the photographer

Pearls of Wisdom

page 198: Woman covering her face: A contemporary piece of jewelry from the Chanel Fine Jewelry collection. Courtesy of Chanel

page 204: La Régente Pearl. Courtesy of Fred Leighton

Bibliography

Books

Aarons, Slim, *A Wonderful Time: An Intimate Portrait of the Good Life.* New York: Harper & Row, 1974.

Abbott, Mary, *Jewels of Romance and Renown.* London: T. W. Laurie, Ltd., 1933.

John T. Alexander, *Catherine the Great: Life and Legend.* New York: Oxford University Press, 1989.

Amory, Cleveland, *Who Killed Society?* New York: Harper, 1960.

Anthony, Katharine, *Catherine the Great.* New York: Alfred A. Knopf, 1926.

Ariès, Philippe and Georges Duby, *A History of Private Life, Volume IV,* Michelle Perot, Editor and Arthur Goldhammer, Translator. Cambridge, MA and London: Belknap Press of Harvard University Press, 1990.

Arnold, Janet, *Queen Elizabeth's Wardrobe Unlock'd.* Leeds, UK: W. S. Maney & Sons, 1988.

Baker, Jean-Claude and Chris Chase, *Josephine.* New York: Random House, 1993.

Baldrige, Letitia, *The Amy Vanderbilt Complete Book of Etiquette: A Guide to Contemporary Living.* Garden City, NY: Doubleday & Company, 1978.

Baldrige, Letitia, *Complete Guide to a Great Social Life.* New York: Rawson Associates, 1987.

Ball, Joanne Dubbs, *Wedding Traditions: Here Comes the Bride.* Dubuque, IA: Antique Trader Books, 1997.

Ballard, Bettina, *In My Fashion.* New York: David McKay, 1960.

Balsan, Consuelo Vanderbilt, *The Glitter and the Gold.* New York: Harper & Brothers Publishers, 1952.

Barrows, Sydney Biddle, *Mayflower Madam.* New York: Arbor House, 1986.

Batterberry, Michael and Ariane, *Fashion: The Mirror of History.* New York: Greenwich House, 1982.

Baudot, François, *Chanel Joaillerie.* Paris: Éditions Assouline, 1998.

Baudot, François, *Chanel: Universe of Fashion.* Paris: Éditions Assouline, 1996.

Beaton, Cecil, *The Glass of Fashion.* Garden City, NY: Doubleday & Company, Inc., 1954.

Beaton, Cecil, *Self-Portrait with Friends,* Richard Buckle, editor. London: Weidenfeld & Nicolson, 1979 and New York: Times Books, 1979.

Bender, Marilyn, *The Beautiful People.* New York: Coward-McCann, 1967.

Birmingham, Stephen, *Jacqueline Bouvier Kennedy Onassis.* New York: Grosset and Dunlap, 1978.

Byron, Stuart and Elizabeth Weis, Editors, *The National Society of Film Critics on Movie Comedy*. New York, Grossman Publishers, 1977.

Calasibetta, Dr. Charlotte, *Fairchild's Dictionary of Fashion*. New York: Fairchild Publications, Inc., 1975.

Callan, Georgina O'Hara, *The Thames and Hudson Dictionary of Fashion Designers*. New York: Thames and Hudson, 1998.

Capote, Truman, *Answered Prayers: The Unfinished Novel*. New York: Random House, 1987.

Capote, Truman, *A Capote Reader*. New York: Random House, 1987.

Cassini, Oleg, *A Thousand Days of Magic: Dressing Jacqueline Kennedy for the White House*. New York: Rizzoli International, 1995.

Castle, Irene, *Castles in the Air*. Garden City, NY: Doubleday, 1958.

Castle, Mrs. Vernon, *My Husband*. New York: Charles Scribner's Sons, 1919.

Charles-Roux, Edmonde, *Chanel and Her World*. New York: The Vendome Press, 1981.

Charles-Roux, Edmonde, *Chanel: Her life, Her World—And the Woman Behind the Legend She Herself Created*. New York: Alfred A. Knopf, Inc., 1975.

Childers, Caroline, Editor, *Prestigious Jewelry*. New York: BW Publications, 1997.

Colette, *Belles Saisons*. [Lausanne]: Mermod, [1947].

Colette, *Cheri/The Last of Cheri*. London: Penguin Books, 1988.

Cooper, Lady Diana, *The Light of Common Day: An Autobiography of Diana Cooper*. London: Century Publishing, 1984.

Core, Philip, *The Original Eye: Arbiters of Twentieth-Century Taste*. London: Quartet Books, 1984.

Coughlan, Robert, *Elizabeth and Catherine, Empresses of All the Russias*. New York: G. P. Putnam's Sons, 1974.

Cumming, Valerie, *Royal Dress*. London: B. T. Batsford, Ltd., 1989.

DeCaro, Frank, *Unmistakably Mackie: The Fashion and Fantasy of Bob Mackie*. New York: Universe Publishing, 1999.

De La Haye, Amy, Shelly Tobin, *Chanel, the Couturière at Work*. Woodstock, NY: The Overlook Press, 1996.

de Montparnasse, Kiki, *Kiki's Memoirs*. Hopewell, NJ: The Ecco Press, 1996.

de Pougy, Liane, *My Blue Notebooks*. New York: Harper & Row Publishers, 1979.

Devi, Gayatri, of Jaipur and Santha Rama Rau. *A Princess Remembers: The Memoirs of the Maharani of Jaipur*. Philadelphia: J. B. Lippincott Company, 1976.

Diliberto, Gioia, *Debutante: The Story of Brenda Frazier*. New York: Knopf, 1987.

Dickinson, Joan Younger, *The Book of Pearls*. New York: Crown, 1968.

Dormann, Geneviève, *Colette: A Passion for Life*. New York: Abbeville Press, 1985.

Eells, George, *Hedda and Louella*. New York: Putnam, 1972.

Eliade, Mircea, *Myths, Rites, Symbols: A Mircea Eliade Reader*. New York: Harper & Row, 1976.

Emrich, Duncan, *The Folklore of Weddings and Marriage: Traditional Beliefs, Customs, Superstitions, Charms and Omens of Marriage and Marriage Ceremonies*. New York: American Heritage Press, 1970.

Erté, *Erté: Things I Remember*. London: Quadrangle/The New York Times Book Co., 1975.

Evans, Joan, *Magical Jewels of the Middle Ages and the Renaissance, Particularly in England*. Oxford: The Clarendon Press, 1922.

Fairchild, John, *Chic Savages*. New York: Simon & Schuster, 1989.

Fairchild, John, *The Fashionable Savages*. Garden City, NY: Doubleday, 1965.

Farn, Alexander, *Pearls: Natural, Cultured, and Imitation*. London: Butterworths, 1986.

Field, Leslie, *The Queen's Jewels: The Personal Collection of Elizabeth II*. New York: Harry N. Abrams, 1987.

Fincher, Jayne and Judy Wade, *Diana: Portrait of a Princess*. New York: Simon & Schuster Editions in association with Callaway Editions, 1998.

Fowler, Marian, *The Way She Looks Tonight*. New York, St. Martin's Press, 1996.

Fox, Patty, *Star Style: Hollywood Legends as Fashion Icons*. Santa Monica, CA: Angel City Press, 1995.

Fraser, Antonia, *The Wives of Henry VIII*. New York: Vintage Books, 1994.

Garner, Philippe and David Alan Mellor, *Cecil Beaton: Photographs 1920-1970*. New York: Stewart, Tabori & Chang, 1994.

Gill, Brendan and Jerome Zerbe, *Happy Times*. New York: Harcourt Brace Jovanovich, 1973.

Giraudoux, Jean, *The Madwoman of Chaillot*, English adaptation by Maurice Valency. Random House, 1947.

Goldsmith, Barbara, *Little Gloria...Happy at Last*. New York: Knopf, 1980.

Grafton, David: *The Sisters*. New York: Villard Books, 1992.

Gross, Elaine and Fred Rottman, *Halston: An American Original*. New York: HarperCollins, 1999.

Gregorietti, Guido, *Jewelry Through the Ages*. New York: American Heritage, 1969.

Haedrich, Marcel, *Coco Chanel: Her Life, Her Secrets*. Boston and Toronto: Little, Brown & Company, 1972.

Hackenbroch, Yvonne, *Renaissance Jewelry*. London: Sotheby Parke Bernet, 1979.

Heiniger, Ernst A. and Jean, *The Great Book of Jewels*. Boston: New York Graphic Society, 1974.

Heymann, C. David, *Poor Little Rich Girl: The Life and Legend of Barbara Hutton*. New York: Random House, 1983.

Hibbert, Christopher, *The Virgin Queen: Elizabeth I, Genius of the Golden Age*. Reading, MA: Addison-Welsley, 1991.

Howell, Georgina, *Diana: Her Life in Fashion*. New York: Rizzoli, 1998.

Hoyt, Edwin Palmer, *The Goulds: A Social History*. New York: Weybright and Talley, 1969.

Hurel, Roselyn and Diana Scarisbrick, *Chaumet Paris: Two Centuries of Fine Jewellery*. Paris: Paris-Musées, Éditions des Musées de la Ville de Paris, 1998.

Jacobson, Stuart E. with text by Jill Spalding, *Only the Best: A Celebration of Gift Giving in America*. New York: Harry N. Abrams, 1985.

Joyce, Kristin and Shellei Addison, *Pearls: Ornament and Obsession*. New York: Simon & Schuster, 1993.

Kazanjian, Dodie, *Icons: The Absolutes of Style*. New York: St. Martin's Press, 1995.

Keller, Helen, *The Story of My Life*. Garden City, NY: Doubleday, 1954.

Kunz, George Frederick, and Charles Hugh Stevenson, *The Book of the Pearl: the History, Art, Science and Industry of the Queen of Gems*. Mineola, NY: Dover Publications, Inc., 1993.

Kunz, George Frederick, *Birth Stones: Natal Stones, Sentiments and Superstitions with Precious Stones*. New York: Tiffany & Co., 1927.

Kunz, George Frederick, *The Curious Lore of Precious Stones*. New York: Dover, 1972.

Lacey, Robert, *Grace*. London: Sidgwick & Jackson, 1994.

Lacey, Robert, *Princess*. London: Bellow & Higton Publishers Ltd, 1982.

Lane, Kenneth Jay and Harrice Simons Miller, *Faking It*. New York: Harry N. Abrams, Inc., 1996.

Laver, James, edited, *Memorable Balls*. London: Derek Verschoyle, 1954.

Latif, Momin, *Bijoux Moghols*. Brussels: La Société, 1982.

Lintilhac, Jean-Paul, *Black Pearls of Tahiti*. Papeete, Tahiti: Royal Tahitian Pearl Book, 1987.

Longford, Elizabeth, *The Queen Mother: A Biography*. New York: William Morrow & Company, Inc., 1981.

Lovell, Mary S., *The Sound of Wings: The Life of Amelia Earhart*. New York: St. Martin's Press, 1989.

Maltin, Leonard, *Movie & Video Guide, 2000*. New York: Penguin Putnam Inc., 1999.

Mascetti, Daniela and Amanda Triossi, *The Necklace: From Antiquity to the Present*. New York: Harry N. Abrams, Inc., 1997.

Massie, Robert K., *Nicholas and Alexandra*. New York: Atheneum, 1967.

Matlins, Antoinette L., *The Pearl Book: The Definitive Buying Guide*. Woodstock, VT: GemStone Press, 1996.

Maugham, W. Somerset, The *Complete Short Stories of Somerset Maugham*. Garden City, NY: Doubleday, 1952.

Mauriès, *Les Bijoux de Chanel*. London: Thames and Hudson, 1993.

Menkes, Suzy, *The Royal Jewels*. London: Grafton Books, 1989.

Menkes, Suzy, *The Windsor Style*. London: Grafton Books, 1987.

Milbank, Caroline Rennolds, *New York Fashion: The Evolution of American Style*. New York: Harry N. Abrams, 1989.

Morris, Michael, *Madame Valentino: The Many Lives of Natacha Rambova*. New York, Abbeville Press, 1991.

Morton, Andrew, *Diana: Her New Life*. New York: Simon & Schuster, 1994.

Mulvagh, Jane, *Costume Jewelry in Vogue*. New York: Thames and Hudson, 1988.

Nadelhoffer, Hans, *Cartier: Jewelers Extraordinary*. New York: Harry N. Abrams, 1984.

Newman, Harold, *An Illustrated Dictionary of Jewelry*. London: Thames & Hudson, 1981.

Newman, Renee, *The Pearl-Buying Guide*. Los Angeles: International Jewelry Publications, 1992.

Onassis, Jacqueline, editor, *In the Russian Style*. New York: the Viking Press, with the cooperation of the Metropolitan Museum of Art, 1976.

Otero, Caroline (La Belle Otero), *My Story*. London: A.M. Philpot, Limited, c. 1927

Pepper, Terence, *High Society: Photographs 1897-1914*. London: National Portrait Gallery Publications, 1998.

Phelps, Robert, *Belles Saisons: A Colette Scrapbook*. New York: Farrar, Straus and Giroux, 1978.

Phillips, Clare, *Jewelry, from Antiquity to the Present*. London: Thames and Hudson, 1996.

Pless, Daisy, Furstin von, *Daisy, Princess of Pless*, New York: E.P. Dutton & Co., Inc., 1929.

Polo, Marco, *Travels of Marco Polo*. New York: Orien Press, 1958.

Proddow, Penny, Debra Healy, Marion Fasel, *Hollywood Jewels*. New York: Harry N. Abrams, Inc., 1992.

Purtell, Joseph, *The Tiffany Touch*. New York: Random House, 1971.

Quine, Judith Balaban, *Bridesmaids: Grace Kelly, Princess of Monaco and Six Intimate Friends*. New York, Weidenfeld & Nicolson, 1989.

Radcliffe, Donnie, *Simply Barbara Bush: A Portrait of America's Candid First Lady*. New York: Warner Books, 1989.

Rich, Doris L., *Amelia Earhart: A Biography*. Washington, D.C.: the Smithsonian Institution, 1989.

Roe, Thomas, Sir, *The Embassy of Sir Thomas Roe to India, 1615-19, as Narrated in his Journal and Correspondence,* Edited by Sir William Foster, C.I.E. London: Oxford University Press, 1926.

Rogers, Alexander (translated); Henry Beveridge (edited), *The Tuzuk-i-Jahangiri (Memoirs Of Jahangir)*. Delhi: Munshisram Manoharlal, Oriental Publishers & Booksellers, Originally published 1909-1914; Second edition, January 1968.

Rosenthal, Leonard, *The Pearl Hunter: An Augobiography*. New York: Schuman, 1952.

Ross, Josephine, Editor, *Beaton in Vogue*. New York: Clarkson N. Potter, 1986.

Ross, Josephine, Editor, *Royalty in Vogue, 1909-1989*. New York: Congdon & Weed, Inc., 1989.

Rudoe, Judy, *Cartier: 1900-1939*. New York: Harry N. Abrams and the Metropolitan Museum of Art, 1997.

Ryersson, Scot D. and Michael Orlando Yaccarino, *Infinite Variety: The Life and Legend of Marchesa Casati*. New York: Viridian Books, 1999.

Sakol, Jeannie and Caroline Latham, *About Grace: An Intimate Notebook*. Chicago: Contemporary Books, Inc., 1993.

Salomon, Paule, and Michel Roudnitska, *Tahiti: The Magic of the Black Pearl*. Tahiti: Tahiti Perles, 1986.

Salway, Lance, *Queen Victoria's Grandchildren*. London: Collins & Brown, 1991.

Scarisbrick, Diana, *Ancestral Jewels*. London: André Deutsch Limited, 1989.

Schiffer, Nancy, *The Power of Jewelry*. West Chester, PA: Schiffer, 1988.

Schumann, Walter, *Gemstones of the World*. New York: Sterling Publishing Co. Inc., 1997.

Spada, James, *Grace: The Secret Life of a Princess*. Garden City, NY: Doubleday & Company, Inc., 1987.

Strong, Roy (evocation) and Julia Trevelyan Oman (spectacle), *Elizabeth R*. New York: Stein and Day, 1972.

Taburiaux, Jean, *Pearls: Their Origin, Treatment and Identification*. Radnor, PA: Chilton Book Co., 1985.

Tapert, Annette and Diana Edkins, *The Power of Style : The Women Who Define the Art of Living Well*. New York: Crown Publishers, Inc., 1994.

Tavernier, Jean Baptiste, *Travels in India*. New Delhi: Oriental Books Reprint Corp., [Exlusively distributed by Munshiram Manoharlal Publishers PVT. LTD. 1977].

Tharp, Louise Hall, *Mrs. Jack: A Biography of Isabella Stewart Gardner*. Boston: Little, Brown & Company, 1965.

Tiffany & Co., *How To Buy A Pearl*, booklet. New York: Tiffany & Company, 1997.

Turnbull, Patrick, *Eugénie of the French*. London: Michael Joseph Ltd., 1974.

Twining, Edward Francis, Lord, *A History of the Crown Jewels of Europe*. London: B. T. Batsford, [1960].

Untracht, Oppi, *Traditional Jewelry of India*. New York: Harry N. Abrams, 1997.

Vickers, Hugo, *Cecil Beaton: A Biography*. New York: Donald I. Fine, Inc., 1985.

Vreeland, Diana, with Christopher Hemphill, *Allure*. Garden City, NY: Doubleday & Company, Inc., 1980.

Vreeland, Diana, *D.V.* New York: Alfred A. Knopf, 1984.

Wallach, Janet, *Chanel: Her Style and Her Life*. New York: Nan A. Talese, 1998.

Ward, Fred*, Pearls*. Bethesda, MD: Gem Book Publishers, 1998.

Ware, Susan, *Amelia Earhart and the Search for Modern Feminism*. New York: W. W. Norton & Company, Inc., 1993.

Young, Sheila, *The Queen's Jewellery*. New York: Taplinger Publishing Company, 1968.

Zucker, Benjamin, *Gems and Jewels: A Connoisseur's Guide*. New York: Thames & Hudson, 1984.

Catalogs

Christie's, *Photographs*. New York: Tuesday, October 5, 1999.

Sotheby's, *The Jewels of the Duchess of Windsor*. Geneva: Thursday April 2 and Friday, April 3, 1987.

Periodicals

Avenue	*New York Post*
Connoisseur	*People*
Country Life	*Quest*
Country Living	*The New Yorker*
Departures	*The New York Observer*
Harper's Bazaar	*The New York Times*
Hello	*Time*
InStyle	*Town and Country*
Modern Jeweler	*Vanity Fair*
National Geographic	*Vogue*
Newsweek	*W*
New York Daily News	*Women's Wear Daily*
New York Observer	

Notes

Front Matter

xiii. "You can't really think. . .": *New York Post*, September 25, 1996; p. 7.

A Quirk of Nature

6. ". . .the crown jewel in the international list. . . .": *The New York Times*, December 8, 1996; p. 65

Innocents

22. ". . . who, before the fifth century (AD), ...": George Frederick Kunz, *The Book of the Pearl* (1927); p. 305.

25. "A baby can't appreciate. . . .": Letitia Baldrige, *The Amy Vanderbilt Complete Book of Etiquette* (1978); pp. 766/767.

32. "A girl's whole life unfolds. . . .": Philippe Ariès and George Duby, *A History of Private Life, Volume IV* (1990); p. 328.

36. After the groom said, "With this ring, I thee wed. . .": Duncan Emrich, *The Folklore of Weddings and Marriage* (1970); p. 32/33.

36. "William was less eager for his daughter's unhappiness. . . .": Stuart E. Jacobson and Jill Spalding, *Only the Best: A Celebration of Gift Giving in America* (1985); p. 93.

Lords & Lovers

45. "The aquiline nose, the pointed. . . .": Cecil Beaton, *Self-Portrait with Friends* (1979); p. 127.

45. "She's highly intelligent. . . .": Diana Vreeland, *Allure* (1980); p. 60.

46. "It is not sufficient. . . .": George Frederick Kunz, *The Book of the Pearl* (1993); p. 9.

50. ". . . already bound to a husband which is the Kingdom of England.": Christopher Hibbert, *The Virgin Queen* (1991); p. 78.

50. "not only ruled. . . .": Christopher Hibbert, *The Virgin Queen* (1991); p. 66.

51. "Why then, if it become not me. . . .": Janet Arnold, *Queen Elizabeth's Wardrobe Unlock'd* (1988); p. 104.

56. ". . . from day to day in unheeded and unrestrained luxury. . . .": Momin Latif, *Bijoux Moghols* (1982); p. 15.

56. ". . . made a hole in his ears and drew into them a shining pearl.": Momin Latif, *Bijoux Moghols* (1982); p. 123-124.

64. "The reign of Napoleon III and his Empress Eugenie. . . .": Michael and Ariane Batterberry, *Fashion: The Mirror of History* (1982 edition); p. 226.

67. ". . . pure like fire, . . .": Philippe Jullian, from an original essay dated April 9th, 1970.

70. ". . . one of my sisters-in-law remarked. . . .": Consuelo Vanderbilt, *The Glitter and the Gold* (1952); p. 185.

Traditionalists

86. "Conservative at first. . . .": Kenneth Jay Lane and Harrice Simons Miller, *Faking It*. New York (1996); p. 142.

97. "Mrs. Gould. . . wore a low-cut. . . .": Edwin P. Hoyt, *The Goulds: A Social History* (1969); p. 195.

98. ". . . showed and taught people. . . .": Mrs. Vernon Castle, *My Husband* (1919); p. 100/101.

101. "She has developed such force of personality. . .": *Beaton in Vogue* (1986), p. 98.

104. "Uptown she was very regal. . . .". Barbara Goldsmith, *Little Gloria, Happy at Last* (1980); p. 208.

106. ". . . received her pearls yet. . . .": Barbara Goldsmith, *Little Gloria, Happy at Last* (1980); p. 102.

106. "In a description that both fits Earhart and rings surprisingly familiar today, *The New York Times* noted. . . .": Susan Ware, *Amelia Earhart and the Search for Modern Feminism* (1993); p. 155 and *The New York Times*, July 24, 1931; pg. 16.

106. "I just don't like shopping very much. I hate ruffles. . . .": Susan Ware, *Amelia Earhart and the Search for Modern Feminism* (1993); p. 99

106. "I had no intention whatever of trying to set a fashion in transatlantic air attire, ...": Susan Ware, *Amelia Earhart and the Search for Modern Feminism* (1993); p. 99.

108. "Her mocking voice. . . .": Regina Marler, *The New York Observer*, July 26, 1999; p. 32.

Dream Makers

118. "A woman needs ropes and ropes of pearls, ...": Courtesy of Chanel.

121. "If there is jewelry, there must be a lot. If it's real. . . .": Marcel Haedrich, *Coco Chanel: Her Life, Her Secrets* (1972), p. 183.

121. "Accessories are what make or mark. . . .": Courtesy of Chanel.

122. "She admitted that nothing was insured. . . .": Bettina Ballard, *In My Fashion* (1960), p. 55.

122. "I'm covered with chokers. . . .": Marcel Haedrich, *Coco Chanel: Her Life, Her Secrets* (1972); p. 182.

122. ". . . in the street. . . .": Marcel Haedrich, *Coco Chanel: Her Life, Her Secrets* (1972); p. 183.

122. "I made false pearls. . . .": Marcel Haedrich, *Coco Chanel: Her Life, Her Secrets* (1972); p. 184.

124. ". . . fantastic glamour. . . .": Diana Vreeland, *D.V.* (1984); p. 33.

125. "Elegance is refusal:" Diana Vreeland, *Allure* (1980); p. 203.

125. "Never fear being vulgar. . . ." Annette Tapert and Diana Edkins, the Power of Style (1994); 142/143.

125. "Actually, on the day she died. . . .": Diana Vreeland, *D.V.* (1984), p. 131.

130. "How many women could be beautiful. . . .": Erté, *Erté: Things I Remember* (1975); p. 76.

130. ". . . all things connected with. . . .": Erté, *Erté: Things I Remember* (1975); p. 11.

130. ". . . the Indian and Persian. . .", Erté, *Erté: Things I Remember* (1975); p. 15.

130. ". . . drew inspiration from. . . ." Erté, *Erté: Things I Remember* (1975); p. 16.

131. "He unbuttoned his pajamas,. . . .": Colette, Cheri/*The Last of Cheri* (1988); p. 15.

153. "It will be the biggest event of the season. . . .": Jack Robertson, *WWD* , (October 24, 1966); p. 28

Untouchables

160. "I am the man. . . .": Robert F. McFadden article, *The New York Times*, May 20, 1994; p. A1.

168. "Suppose I said your pearls were false. . . .": Jean Giraudoux, *The Mad Woman of Chaillot* (1947); p. 86.

169. "Everyone knows. . . .": Jean Giraudoux, *The Madwoman of Chaillot* (1947); p. 86.

170. ". . . fashion entered politics. . .": John Fairchild, *The Fashionable Savages* (1965); p 119.

175. ". . . love of words. . .": John F. Kennedy, Jr. tribute reported by Janny Scott, *The New York Times*, (May 24, 1994), p. A16.

177. ". . . seemed so composed,. . .": Robert Lacey, *Princess* (1982); p. 11.

180. "Diana's appeal as a postmodern icon. . . ." Cathy Horyn, *Vanity Fair*, July 1997, p. 72.

180. "First it was demure Di, ...'": Judy Wade to Joan Juliet Buck, *Vanity Fair*, December (1989), p. 219

Eternal Lights

186. "For a swan is. . . .": Truman Capote, *A Capote Reader* (1987); p. 551.

188. "Babe Paley gives the impression. . . .": John Fairchild, *The Fashionable Savages* (1965), p. 147.

188. "She couldn't be more. . . .": John Fairchild, *The Fashionable Savages* (1965), p. 147.

190. ". . . she is the only woman. . . .": John Fairchild, *The Fashionable Savages* (1965), p. 148.

196. ". . . crown jewels of New York City. . . .:" Brendan Gill, *New Yorker*, April 21, 1997; p. 76.

Pearls of Wisdom

202. "To check luster, stand. . . .": Tiffany & Co., *How to Buy a Pearl* (1997), p. 6.